STL
Pocket Reference

STL
Pocket Reference

Ray Lischner

Beijing · Cambridge · Farnham · Köln · Paris · Sebastopol · Taipei · Tokyo

STL Pocket Reference

by Ray Lischner

Published by O'Reilly Media, Inc., 1005 Gravenstein Highway North,
Sebastopol, CA 95472.

O'Reilly & Associates books may be purchased for educational,
business, or sales promotional use. Online editions are also available
for most titles (*safari.oreilly.com*). For more information, contact our
corporate/institutional sales department: (800) 998-9938 or
corporate@oreilly.com.

Editor:	Jonathan Gennick
Production Editor:	Marlowe Shaeffer
Cover Designer:	Ellie Volckhausen
Interior Designer:	David Futato

Printing History:

October 2003:   First Edition.

0-596-00556-3
[C]   [3/04]

Contents

STL Pocket Reference

Introduction

STL Pocket Reference is a quick reference to the Standard Template Library portion of the standard C++ library, as documented in ISO/IEC 14882:2003(E), *Programming Languages—C++*, which is the original 1998 standard plus the corrections and additions in Technical Corrigendum 1.

The name Standard Template Library (STL) does not appear in the C++ standard, and the STL is not a formal part of the standard. Instead, the term STL usually refers to that part of the standard library that owes its heritage to the original STL, written by Alexander Stepanov, David Musser, and Meng Lee of Hewlett-Packard in the early 1990s, based on earlier work in Ada. Their innovative library of generic algorithms, iterators, and containers was quickly adopted as part of the C++ standard. The templates that were once the STL evolved and changed as the standard moved toward completion in 1998. Some other parts of the library, such as the basic_string class template, were changed to be more container-like, even though they were not part of the original STL.

This book describes what the STL has become: the algorithms, iterators, and containers in the standard C++ library, plus other relevant bits and pieces. For example, bitset<> is not a standard container, but it is included because the standard lists it in the same section as the containers and because it is useful.

The last section in this book discusses the Boost project, which is not part of the C++ standard library but is important for all C++ users. It includes several libraries that extend and enhance the STL.

The purpose of this book, as with any Pocket Reference, is to remind you of what you already know. That is, you should already know how to use algorithms, iterators, and containers. This book is a concise reference to remind you of the specific functions, classes, templates, and member functions that make up the STL. If you need a detailed reference, see *C++ in a Nutshell*. If you want to learn C++ or the STL, visit the book's web site (*http://www.tempest-sw.com/cpp*) for information about other books that are suitable for instruction.

This book is a companion to the *C++ Pocket Reference*, which covers the C++ language, but not the library. You might also want to consult the *C Pocket Reference*, which includes information about the C standard library, part of the C++ standard library.

In order to keep this book down to Pocket Reference size, it does not cover C++ I/O streams, numerics, or other parts of the C++ standard library. Nor does it offer much advice on the proper use of the STL. See the book's web site (*http://www.tempest-sw.com/cpp*) for other book recommendations.

Conventions Used in This Book

This book uses the following typographic conventions:

Italic
> Used for filenames, URLs, emphasis, and for the first use of a technical term.

Constant Width
> Used for identifiers and symbols.

Constant Width Italic
> Used for names that are not specified by the standard, such as hidden names of temporary objects.

Constant Width Bold
> Used in complex declarations to highlight the name being declared. In some C++ declarations, especially for templates, the name gets buried in the middle of the declaration and can be hard to spot.

In this book, the mathematical notation of [*first*, *last*) is often used to denote a range. The square bracket marks an inclusive endpoint of a range, and the parenthesis marks an exclusive endpoint of a range. Thus, [*first*, *last*) means a range that extends from *first* to *last*, including *first* but excluding *last*. Read more about ranges in the "Iterators" section later in this book.

Every function, class, and template in the STL, like the rest of the standard library, resides in the std namespace. This book omits the std:: qualifier from declarations, descriptions, and most examples for the sake of brevity.

Acknowledgments

I thank my editor, Jonathan Gennick, and my technical reviewers, Reed Hedges and Andrew Duncan. I could not have written this book without the support and understanding of my wife, Cheryl, and son, Arthur.

Containers

The C++ library has a basic suite of container types (deques, lists, maps, sets, and vectors), which are described in this section. This section also discusses the basic_string class template because it is like a container. The non-container bitset template is covered in the later section, "Miscellaneous." The fundamental purpose of a container is to store multiple objects in a single container object. Different kinds of containers have different characteristics: speed, size, and ease of use. The choice of container depends on the characteristics and behavior you require.

To add items to a container, call an `insert` member function. You can also use `push_back` or `push_front`, if they are available. Some containers offer additional means of adding items, such as `map::operator[]`.

To remove items from a container, call an `erase` member function, or a specialized version such as `pop_back` or `pop_front`. Some containers offer additional means of removing items, such as `list::remove`.

NOTE

Note that the standard algorithms (see "Algorithms") cannot erase items from a container. Instead, the `remove` and related algorithms reorganize the elements of a sequence in preparation for calling `erase`.

Standard Containers

The standard containers fall into two categories: sequence and associative containers. A sequence container preserves the original order in which items were added to the container. An associative container keeps items in ascending order (you can define the order relation) to speed up searching.

Sequence containers

The sequence containers are:

`basic_string`
`string`
`wstring`

> These containers represent character strings. The string class templates are not usually considered standard containers, but they meet most of the requirements of a sequence container. The header is `<string>`.

deque

> A deque (double-ended queue) supports fast (constant complexity) insertions and deletions at the beginning and end of the container. Inserting or deleting at any other position is slower (linear complexity), but random access to any item is fast. Items are not stored contiguously. The header is <deque>.

list

> A list supports rapid insertion or deletion at any position but does not support random access. Items are not stored contiguously. The header is <list>.

vector

> A vector is like an array, except that the vector can grow as needed. Items can be rapidly added or removed only at the end. At other positions, inserting and deleting items is slower. Random access to any item is fast. Items are stored contiguously. The header is <vector>.

Associative containers

The associative containers are:

map
multimap

> A map (or dictionary) is an associative container that stores pairs of keys and associated objects. Pairs are stored in ascending order of keys. A map requires unique keys. A multimap permits duplicate keys. The header for map and multimap is <map>.

set
multiset

> A set is an associative container that stores keys in ascending order. A set requires unique keys. A multiset permits duplicate keys. The header for set and multiset is <set>.

The set and map containers perform insertions, deletions, and searches with logarithmic complexity.

Container Adapters

In addition to the standard containers, the standard library has several container adapters. An adapter is a class template that uses a container for storage and provides a restricted interface when compared with the standard containers. Adapters do not have iterators, so they cannot be used with the standard algorithms. The standard adapters are:

priority_queue
> A priority queue is organized so that the largest element is always the first. You can add an item to the queue, examine the first element, or remove the first element. The header is <queue>.

queue
> A queue is a sequence of elements that lets you add elements at one end and remove them at the other end. This organization is commonly known as FIFO (first-in, first-out). The header is <queue>.

stack
> A stack is a sequence that lets you add and remove elements only at one end. This organization is commonly known as LIFO (last-in, first-out). The header is <stack>.

Values

In C++, the containers are implemented as class templates. The first template parameter is the type of the objects that are to be stored in the container. You can use any type that has *value semantics*, which means objects must behave as ordinary values in the same manner as integers or other fundamental types. Values can be copied and assigned freely. An original and its copy must compare as equal.

Sequence containers compare objects for equality with the == operator. Associative containers compare objects for *equivalence*, which is slightly different from equality. Two objects,

A and B, are equivalent if A < B is false and B < A is false. You can substitute a different function or functor for the < operator, provided it implements a meaningful comparison (called *strict weak ordering* in the standard). In particular, A < A is always false, and if A < B and B < C, then A < C.

Associative containers take an additional template parameter for the comparison function or functor. The default is always less<>, which compares objects using the < operator. Some associative containers require unique keys, while others permit duplicate keys. Uniqueness is determined by testing for equivalence, not equality.

Common Members

This section presents the members that are common to the standard containers. Subsequent sections present the specifics for each container type. Some members are found in every container type, some in sequence containers only, and others in associative containers only. Each of these categories is covered in its own subsection.

Member types

Every container declares the following member typedefs:

allocator_type
    A synonym for the Allocator template parameter.

const_iterator
    The iterator type for const values.

const_pointer
    A synonym for the allocator's const_pointer type.

const_reference
    A const lvalue type for the items stored in the container. Typically the same as the allocator's const_reference type.

difference_type
> A signed integral type denoting the difference between two iterators.

iterator
> The iterator type.

pointer
> A synonym for the allocator's pointer type.

reference
> An lvalue type for the items stored in the container. This is typically the same as the allocator's reference type.

size_type
> An unsigned integral type that can hold any non-negative difference_type value.

value_type
> The type of item stored in the container. This is typically the same as the first template parameter.

A container that supports bidirectional iterators also defines the reverse_iterator and const_reverse_iterator types. These are iterators that run in the reverse direction, from the last item to the first.

An associative container defines key_type as the key type, compare_type as the type of the key compare function or functor, and value_compare as the type of a function or functor that compares two value_type objects.

Constructors and destructor

A container template has the constructors outlined in the following list. Whether the constructors are implemented using overloading or default arguments is unimportant and left to the implementation. If you supply an allocator object, it is copied to the container; otherwise, a default allocator is constructed. In each of the following descriptions, ***container*** is the name of the container class template.

container( )
container(allocator_type)
> Constructs an empty container. Complexity is constant.

container(const container& that)
> Constructs a container with a copy of all the items and the allocator from that. Complexity is linear.

A sequence container has the following additional constructors:

container(size_type n, const value_type& x)
container(size_type n, const value_type& x,
          allocator_type)
> Constructs a container that has n copies of x. Complexity is linear with respect to n.

template<typename InIter>
container(InIter first, InIter last)
template<typename InIter>
container(InIter first, InIter last,allocator_type)
> Constructs a container with copies of the items in the range [first, last). Complexity is linear.

> If InIter is an integral type, the container is initialized with first copies of last (converted to value_type). Complexity is linear.

An associative container has the following additional constructors:

container(key_compare compare)
container(key_compare compare, allocator_type)
> Constructs an empty container that uses compare to compare keys. Complexity is constant.

```
template<typename Inp>
container(Inp first, Inp last, key_compare compare)
template<typename Inp>
container(Inp first, Inp last, key_compare compare,
         allocator_type)
```
> Constructs a container with copies of the items in the range [first, last), comparing keys with compare. Complexity is linear.

All containers have a destructor:

~container( )
> Calls the destructor for every object in the container, which is equivalent to calling clear( ). Complexity is linear.

Common member functions

The following member functions are common to all container types:

```
iterator begin( )
const_iterator begin( ) const
```
> Returns an iterator that points to the first item of the container. Complexity is constant.

```
void clear( )
```
> Erases all the items in the container. Complexity is linear.

```
bool empty( ) const
```
> Returns true if the container is empty (size( ) == 0). Complexity is constant.

```
iterator end( )
const_iterator end( ) const
```
> Returns an iterator that points to one position past the last item of the container. Complexity is constant.

erase(iterator p)
> Erases the item that p points to. For a sequence container, erase returns an iterator that points to the item that comes immediately after the deleted item or end( ). Complexity depends on the container.

For an associative container, erase does not return a value. Complexity is constant (amortized over many calls).

erase(iterator first, iterator last)
Erases all the items in the range [first, last). For a sequence container, erase returns an iterator that points to the item that comes immediately after the last deleted item or end( ). Complexity depends on the container.

For an associative container, erase does not return a value. Complexity is logarithmic, plus the number of items erased.

allocator_type **get_allocator**( ) const
Returns a copy of the allocator object.

size_type **max_size**( ) const
Returns the largest number of items the container can possibly hold. Complexity is usually constant.

container& **operator=**(const container& that)
Erases all items from this container and then copies all the items from that. Returns *this. Complexity is linear.

reverse_iterator **rbegin**( )
const_reverse_iterator **rbegin**( ) const
Returns a reverse iterator that points to the last item of the container. Complexity is constant.

reverse_iterator **rend**( )
const_reverse_iterator **rend**( ) const
Returns a reverse iterator that points to one position before the first item of the container. Complexity is constant.

size_type **size**( ) const
Returns the number of items in the container. Complexity is usually constant. (See the "Lists" section for when complexity is not constant.)

```
void swap(const container& that)
```
   Swaps the elements of this container with that. Associa-
   tive containers also swap their comparison functions.
   Complexity is usually constant.

All containers have the equality and relational operators
defined, either as member functions or as functions at the
namespace level. The std::swap function is overloaded to call
the swap member function when swapping two container
objects of the same type.

Optional member functions

The following functions are optional. The standard containers provide only those functions that have constant complexity (possibly amortized over many calls). The containers that
define these functions are shown in parentheses.

```
reference at(size_type n)
const_reference at(size_type n) const
```
   Returns the item at index n, or throws out_of_range if n
   >= size( ). (basic_string, deque, vector)

```
reference back( )
const_reference back( ) const
```
   Returns the last item in the container. Behavior is undefined if the container is empty. (deque, list, vector)

```
reference front( )
const_reference front( ) const
```
   Returns the first item in the container. Behavior is undefined if the container is empty. (deque, list, vector)

```
reference operator[](size_type n)
const_reference operator[](size_type n) const
```
   Returns the item at index n. Behavior is undefined if n >=
   size( ). If n=size(), the behavior is undefined for most
   containers. The exception is basic_string, which returns
   a null character. (basic_string, deque, vector)

void **pop_back**( )
> Erases the last item in the container. Behavior is undefined if the container is empty. (deque, list, vector)

void **pop_front**( )
> Erases the first item in the container. Behavior is undefined if the container is empty. (deque, list)

void **push_back**(const value_type& x)
> Inserts x as the new last item in the container. (basic_string, deque, list, vector)

void **push_front**(const value_type& x)
> Inserts x as the new first item in the container. (deque, list)

Sequence member functions

All sequence containers define the following member functions. Unless otherwise indicated, the complexity of each depends on the container type.

template <typename InputIterator>
void **assign**(InputIterator first, InputIterator last)
> Replaces the container's contents with the items in the range [first, last) unless InputIterator is an integral type, in which case the arguments are interpreted as though they were cast as follows:

```
assign(static_cast<size_type>(first),
       static_cast<value_type>(last));
```

> Complexity is always linear.

void **assign**(size_type n, const T& value)
> Replaces the container's contents with n copies of value. Complexity is always linear.

iterator **insert**(iterator p, const value_type& x)
> Inserts x immediately before p and returns an iterator that points to x.

```
void insert(iterator p, size_type n, const value_type& x)
```
Inserts n copies of x before p.

```
template<typename InIter>
void insert(iterator p, InIter first, InIter last)
```
Copies the values from [first, last) and inserts them before p.

Associative member functions

All associative containers define the member functions discussed in the following list. In the descriptions of complexity, N refers to the number of elements in the container, M refers to the number of elements in the argument range (e.g., last − first), and *count* is the value that the function returns. Some of these member functions seem to duplicate standard algorithms (as discussed under the later section, "Algorithms"), but the associative containers can implement the member functions with better performance than the generic algorithms.

```
size_type count(const key_type& k) const
```
Returns the number of items equivalent to k. Complexity is $\log N + count$.

```
pair<const_iterator,const_iterator>
equal_range(const key_type& k) const
pair<iterator,iterator> equal_range(const key_type& k)
```
Returns the lower and upper bounds of a key. It is equivalent to calling make_pair(lower_bound(k), upper_bound(k)). Complexity is $\log N$.

```
size_type erase(const key_type& k)
```
Erases all the items equivalent to k. Returns the number of items erased. Complexity is $\log N + count$.

```
const_iterator find(const key_type& k) const
iterator find(const key_type& k)
```
Finds an item equivalent to k and returns an iterator that points to one such item, or end( ) if no such item is found. Complexity is $\log N$.

---

insert(const value_type& x)

> Inserts x. If the container permits duplicate keys, insert returns an iterator that points to the newly inserted item. If the container requires unique keys, insert returns pair<iterator,bool>, where the first element of the pair is an iterator that points to an item equivalent to x, and the second element is true if x was inserted or false if x was already present in the container. Complexity is log N.

iterator **insert**(iterator p, const value_type& x)

> Inserts x and returns an iterator that points to x. The iterator p is a hint as to where x might belong. Complexity is log N in general, but is amortized constant if the hint is correct; that is, if x is inserted immediately after p.

template<typename InIter> void
insert(InIter first, InIter last)

> Copies the items from [first, last) and inserts each item in the container. Complexity is $M \log(N + M)$, but is linear if the range is already sorted.

key_compare **key_comp**( ) const

> Returns the key compare function or functor. Complexity is constant.

const_iterator **lower_bound**(const key_type& k) const
iterator **lower_bound**(const key_type& k)

> Returns an iterator that points to the first item in the set that does not come before k. That is, the iterator points to the position of its first occurrence if k is in the container; otherwise, the iterator points to the first position where k should be inserted. Complexity is log N.

value_compare **value_comp**( ) const

> Returns the value compare function or functor. Complexity is constant.

```
const_iterator upper_bound(const key_type& k) const
iterator upper_bound(const key_type& k)
```
Returns an iterator that points to the first item in the container that comes after all occurrences of k. Complexity is log N.

Exceptions

The standard containers are designed to be robust in the face of exceptions. The exceptions that the containers themselves can throw are well-defined (for example, at might throw out_of_range), and most member functions do not throw any exceptions of their own.

If a single value is being added to a container (by calling insert, push_front, or push_back), and an exception is thrown, the container remains in a valid state without adding the value to the container.

When inserting more than one value, different containers have different behaviors. A list, for example, ensures that all items are inserted or that none are; that is, if an exception is thrown, the list is unchanged. A deque and vector behave similarly, and if an exception is thrown, such as bad_alloc, the container is unchanged. If the exception is thrown from the value type's copy constructor or assignment operator, however, the behavior is undefined.

A map or set ensures only that each individual item is inserted successfully. If an exception is thrown after inserting some of the items from a range, the destination container retains the elements that had been inserted successfully.

The erase, pop_back, and pop_front functions never throw exceptions.

The swap function throws an exception only if an associative container's Compare object's copy constructor or assignment operator throws an exception.

Deques

A deque (double-ended queue) is a sequence container that supports rapid insertion and deletion at both ends of the sequence, so it has the `back`, `front`, and related member functions. A deque permits random access with constant complexity, so it has the `at` member function, `operator[]`, and random access iterators.

After inserting at the beginning or end of the deque, all iterators become invalid. All references and pointers to items in the deque remain valid. After inserting in the middle of the deque, all iterators, references, and pointers to items in the deque become invalid.

After erasing an element from the beginning or end of the deque, all iterators and references remain valid except those pointing to the erased element. After erasing an element from the middle of the deque, all iterators, references, and pointers to items in the deque become invalid.

The `deque<T, Allocator>` class template supports all the standard members for a sequence container, plus the following:

explicit **deque**(size_type n)
> Constructs a deque with n copies of T( ).

void **resize**(size_type n, T t = T( ))
> Changes the size of the deque to n. If n > size( ), one or more copies of t are added to the end of the deque to reach the desired size. If the new size is smaller than the current size, the first n elements are unchanged, and elements are erased from the end to reach the new size.

The deque class template implements all of the optional member functions:

at	pop_back
back	pop_front
front	push_back
operator[]	push_front

Lists

A list is a sequence container that supports constant complexity insertion and deletion at any position. Indexing, however, requires linear complexity. Thus, a list supports bidirectional iterators but not random access iterators. A doubly linked list is the typical implementation of the list container.

When an item is erased from a list (by calling clear, erase, remove, pop_back, etc.), all iterators that point to that item become invalid, as do all pointers and references to the item. No other iterators, pointers, or references are invalidated when inserting or erasing any items.

NOTE

The size function can have constant or linear complexity. The standard encourages library vendors to implement the list class template so that size has constant complexity, but it permits worse performance (namely, linear in the size of the list). If size does not have constant complexity, you should expect all versions of splice to have constant complexity in all cases. (This last constraint is mandated not by the standard but by common sense.)

The list<T, Allocator> class template supports all the standard members for a sequence container, plus the following:

explicit **list**(size_type n)
  Constructs a list that contains n copies of T( ).

void **merge**(list<T,Alloc>& x)
template <class Compare>
void **merge**(list<T,Alloc>& x, Compare comp)
  Merges another sorted list, x, into this list, which must also be sorted. Items are erased from x, so after merge returns, x is empty. Items are compared using the < operator or comp. The same function that was used to sort the items must be used to compare the items. The merge is

---

stable, so the relative order of items is unchanged; if the same item is already in the list and in x, the item from x is added after the item already in the list.

The performance of the merge is linear: exactly size( ) + x.size( ) - 1 comparisons are performed.

void **remove**(const T& value)

    Erases all occurrences of value from the list. The performance is linear: exactly size( ) comparisons are performed.

template <typename Predicate>
void **remove_if**(Predicate pred)

    Erases all items for which pred(*item*) returns true. The performance is linear: pred is called exactly size( ) times.

void **resize**(size_type sz, T t = T( ))

    Changes the size of the list to n. If n > size( ), one or more copies of t are added to the end of the list to reach the desired size. If the new size is smaller than the current size, elements are erased from the end to reach the new size.

void **reverse**( )

    Reverses the order of the entire list. The performance is linear.

void **sort**( )
template <typename Compare> void **sort**(Compare comp)

    Sorts the items in the list, comparing items with the < operator or by calling comp. The sort is stable, so the relative positions of items do not change. The performance is $N \log N$ where N is size( ).

NOTE

You must call the sort member function to sort a list. The generic sort algorithm requires a random access iterator, but list provides only a bidirectional iterator.

```
void splice(iterator pos, list<T,Alloc>& x)
void splice(iterator pos, list<T,Alloc>& x, iterator i)
void splice(iterator pos, list<T,Alloc>& x,
            iterator first, iterator last)
```

Moves one or more items from x to the list, inserting the items just before pos. The first form moves every item from x to the list. The second form moves the item at position i. The third form moves all items in the range [first, last). If *this and x are the same container, pos must not be in the range [first, last).

The complexity of the third form is not linear when &x != this; all other cases work with constant complexity. If size has linear complexity, you should expect splice to have constant complexity in all cases.

```
void unique( )
template <typename BinPred> void unique(BinPred pred)
```

Erases adjacent duplicate items from the list. Items are compared with the == operator or by calling pred. When adjacent equal items are found in the list, the first one is retained and the second and subsequent items are erased. The performance is linear.

The list class template implements the following optional member functions:

back	pop_front
front	push_back
pop_back	push_front

Maps

A map is an associative container that offers insertion and deletion of keys in logarithmic time. Each key maps to an associated object. The map<Key, T, Compare, Allocator> type requires unique keys, and multimap<Key, T, Compare, Allocator> permits duplicate keys.

Each key/object combination is stored as a `pair<const Key, T>` (which is the definition of `value_type`). A map's iterators are bidirectional. They return `value_type` references; use the `first` member of `pair<>` to access the key and the `second` to access the associated object.

Note that keys are const in the map. You must not change a key while it is stored in a map. More precisely, you must not change a key in a way that alters its relative order with the other keys in the map. If you need to modify a key, erase the key from the map, modify the key, and insert the new key with its original associated value.

Within a map, keys are in ascending order, according to the `Compare` template parameter (which can be a function pointer or functor that compares two objects of type `Key` and returns true if the first argument should come before the second). The uniqueness of keys is determined only by calling `Compare`, not by using the `==` operator. That is, two objects, `a` and `b`, are different (and therefore can both be present in a single map object) if `Compare(a, b)` is true or `Compare(b, a)` is true.

Inserting into a map does not invalidate any iterators, pointers, or references for that map. Erasing an element invalidates only iterators, pointers, and references that refer to that element.

Insertion into a map and searching for an element in a map usually have logarithmic complexity. Erasing a single element, given an iterator, has amortized constant complexity.

The `map` and `multimap` class templates support all the standard members for an associative container, plus `mapped_type`, a synonym for the second template parameter, which is the type of the associated objects. The `map` template (but not `multimap`) also defines the following:

```
T& operator[](const key_type& x)
```
The subscript operator returns a reference to the object associated with the key x. If x is not in the map, it is added with a default associated object, and a reference to that new object is returned.

That is, operator[] returns the following:

```
(*((insert(std::make_pair(x, T()))).first)).second
```
Note that there is no const version of this operator.

Priority Queues

A priority queue is a restricted queue that keeps the largest (highest priority) value at the top of the queue. The only operations are to add an item to the queue, examine the top item, or remove the top item.

The priority_queue<T, Container, Compare> class template is an adapter for any sequence container that supports random access, such as deque and vector. (The default is vector.) The priority queue keeps its elements in heap order (see "Heap Operations" in the later section, "Algorithms"), so it requires a comparator (the Compare template parameter). The default comparator is less<T>.

Unlike queue, priority_queue has no relational or equality operators.

Most of the members of priority_queue are straightforward mappings from a simple queue protocol to the underlying container protocol. The members are:

```
explicit priority_queue(const Compare& cmp = Compare(),
                        const Container& cont =
                        Container())
```
Constructs a queue that contains a copy of cont, using cmp as the comparison function. Then calls make_heap to initialize the priority queue. Complexity is linear.

```
template <typename Inp>
priority_queue(Inp first, Inp last, const
               Compare& cmp = Compare( ), const
               Container& cont = Container( ))
```
Constructs a queue that contains a copy of cont using cmp as the comparison function. Then copies the items from the range [first, last) to the queue. Finally calls make_heap to initialize the priority queue. Complexity is linear.

bool **empty**( ) const
Returns true if the priority queue is empty. Complexity is constant.

void **pop**( )
Erases the largest (last) item from the priority queue by calling pop_heap and then erases the last element in the container. Complexity is logarithmic.

void **push**(const value_type& x)
Inserts x in the container and then calls push_heap to ensure the priority queue order. Complexity is logarithmic.

size_type **size**( ) const
Returns the number of items in the priority queue. Complexity is usually constant.

const value_type& **top**( ) const
Returns the largest (last) item in the priority queue. Complexity is constant.

Queues

A queue is a sequence that permits insertion at one end and deletion from the other end. Because the first item inserted into a queue is the first item removed, a queue is sometimes called a FIFO container.

The queue<T,Container> class template is an adapter for any sequence container, such as deque and list, that supports the front, back, push_back, and pop_front members. (The default is deque.)

All the relational and equality operators (==, >, etc.) are defined to compare queue objects by comparing the adapted containers' contents.

Most of the members of queue are straightforward mappings from a simple queue protocol to the underlying container protocol. The members are:

explicit **queue**(const Container& cont = Container( ))

Takes an existing container cont and copies its contents into the queue. With no argument, the constructor creates a new, empty container for the queue. Complexity is linear.

value_type& **back**( )
const value_type& **back**( ) const

Returns the last item in the queue, that is, the item that was added most recently to the queue. Complexity is constant.

bool **empty**( ) const

Returns true if the queue is empty. Complexity is constant.

value_type& **front**( )
const value_type& **front**( ) const

Returns the first item in the queue. Complexity is constant.

void **pop**( )

Erases the first item from the queue. Complexity is constant.

void **push**(const value_type& x)

Inserts x at the end of the queue. Complexity is constant.

size_type **size**( ) const

Returns the number of items in the queue. Complexity is usually constant.

Sets

A set is an associative container that stores keys in ascending order. The set<Key, Compare, Allocator> class template

---

stores unique keys, and multiset<Key, Compare, Allocator> permits duplicate keys.

A set's iterators are bidirectional. Note that keys are const in the set. You must not change a key while it is stored in a set. More precisely, you must not change a key in a way that alters its relative order with the other keys in the set. If you need to modify a key, first erase the key from the set. Then modify the key and insert the new key.

Within a set, keys are in ascending order according to the Compare template parameter (which can be a function pointer or functor that compares two objects of type Key and returns true if the first argument should come before the second). When searching for keys, they are compared using the function or functor specified by the Compare template parameter. Two objects, a and b, are different if Compare(a, b) is true or Compare(b, a) is true.

Inserting into a set does not invalidate any iterators, pointers, or references for that set. Erasing an element invalidates only iterators, pointers, and references that refer to that element.

Insertion into a set and searching for an element in a set usually have logarithmic complexity. Erasing a single element, given an iterator, has constant complexity, amortized over many erasures.

The set and multiset class templates support all the standard member functions of an associative container and do not define any additional members.

Stacks

A stack is a sequence of items that supports insertion and removal at one end. Because the last item inserted into a stack is the first item removed, a stack is sometimes called a LIFO container.

The stack class template is an adapter for any sequence container, such as deque, list, and vector, that supports the back, push_back, and pop_back members. (The default is deque.)

All the relational and equality operators (==, >, etc.) are defined to compare stack objects by comparing the adapted containers' contents.

Most of the members of stack<T, Container> are straightforward mappings from a simple stack protocol to the underlying container protocol. The members are:

explicit **stack**(const Container& cont = Container( ))
    Constructs the stack by copying the elements from cont. Complexity is linear.

bool **empty**( ) const
    Returns true if the stack is empty. Complexity is constant.

void **pop**( )
    Erases the item at the top of the stack. Complexity is constant.

void **push**(const value_type& x)
    Adds x at the top of the stack. Complexity is constant.

size_type **size**( ) const
    Returns the number of items in the stack. Complexity is usually constant.

value_type& **top**( )
const value_type& **top**( ) const
    Returns the item at the top of the stack. Complexity is constant.

Strings

The basic_string class template is used for the standard string types:

typedef basic_string<char> string
    Represents a narrow character string.

typedef basic_string<wchar_t> wstring
    Represents a wide character string.

A string is a sequence of characters that provides a number of useful member functions for searching and modifying the string. The basic_string template is very much like a sequence container, and it has the same members as the standard sequence containers, including at and operator[], but not front, back, or pop_back. Strings support random access iterators. String contents are not necessarily stored contiguously; see the c_str and data member functions if you need the string contents as a contiguous character array.

If you have a sequence of characters that you don't need to treat as a character string, you can use vector<char> or vector<wchar_t>, but in most cases you will probably find string or wstring to be more convenient. You can usually use a string or wstring as a container that supports random access iterators, so you can use strings with the standard algorithms.

Many of the member functions can throw exceptions. Specifying an index out of range throws out_of_range (except operator[] does not throw an exception). An attempt to construct a string or modify a string so its length exceeds max_size( ) throws length_error. The basic_string class uses an allocator object for memory allocation, which can throw an exception (such as bad_alloc) almost any time the string is modified.

Iterators, pointers, and references to elements of a string become invalid in the following situations:

- The string is the target of the swap member function or an argument to the swap function template.
- The string is an argument to operator>> or getline.
- You call the data or c_str member function.
- You call any non-const member function except operator[], at, begin, end, rbegin, or rend.
- You call the non-const version of operator[], at, begin, end, rbegin, or rend after any of the above situations, except after calling a form of insert or erase that returns an iterator (so that the returned iterator remains valid).

The `basic_string<charT, Traits, Alloc>` class template requires an additional template parameter: the character traits. The `string` and `wstring` classes use the standard `char_traits` class template, which describes the characteristics, or traits, of a character type and provides basic policies for comparing characters, copying character arrays, and so on. (The `char_traits` template is not covered in this book because most STL users rely on the default implementation.)

In addition to the standard type members, `basic_string` declares the following `typedef`:

`traits_type`
    A synonym for the character traits.

The `basic_string` class template has a single public data member:

`static const size_type npos = -1`
    Returned from some functions to indicate an error or "not found." Used as a size argument to mean "maximum size" or a position argument to mean "maximum position."

The `basic_string` class template supports all the standard members of a sequence container, plus the members outlined in the following list. Several small examples appear throughout this section, illustrating the use of some of the more complex member functions. Some of the functions are described in terms of temporary string objects or calls to other member functions. The use of temporaries is only to help describe the member function's behavior. The actual implementation is not required to use a temporary object, and good implementations avoid creating unnecessary temporary strings.

basic_string(const basic_string& str, size_type pos,
              size_type n = npos, const Alloc& a = Alloc( ))
    Copies a substring of str, starting at pos. If pos is out of range (that is, pos > str.size( )), out_of_range is thrown.

The number of characters copied is n or the number of characters left in the string (str.size() - pos), whichever is smaller.

basic_string(const charT* s, size_type n,
            const Alloc& a = Alloc())
Copies the first n characters from s.

basic_string(const charT* s, const Alloc& a = Alloc())
Copies a null-terminated character array, s.

basic_string& **append**(const basic_string& str,
                    size_type pos, size_type n)
Appends characters to the end of this string. If pos > str.size(), out_of_range is thrown. Otherwise, up to n characters are copied from str, starting at position pos. The return value is *this.

basic_string& **append**(const basic_string& str)
Returns append(str, 0, npos).

basic_string& **append**(const charT* s, size_type n)
basic_string& **append**(const charT* s)
basic_string& **append**(size_type n, charT c)
template<class InputIter>
basic_string& **append**(InputIter first, InputIter last)
Constructs a temporary string *tmp*, passes the arguments to the constructor, and returns append(*tmp*).

basic_string& **assign**(const basic_string& str,
                    size_type pos, size_type n)
Erases the current contents of this string and replaces them with the substring of str that starts at pos and extends for up to n characters. The return value is *this.

basic_string& **assign**(const basic_string& str)
Returns assign(str, 0, npos).

```
basic_string& assign(const charT* s, size_type n)
basic_string& assign(const charT* s)
basic_string& assign(size_type n, charT c)
template<class InputIter>
basic_string& assign(InputIter first, InputIter last)
```
Constructs a temporary string *tmp*, passes the arguments to the constructor, and returns assign(*tmp*).

```
reference at(size_type n)
const_reference at(size_type n) const
```
Returns the character at index n, or throws out_of_range if n >= size( ).

```
const charT* c_str( ) const
```
Returns a pointer to a null-terminated (C-style) character array that contains the same characters as this string, followed by a terminating null character. You should not modify the contents of the returned character array. The pointer becomes invalid after calling any non-const member function of the string. The typical use of c_str is to interface with C functions that require a null-terminated character array:

```
    std::printf(fmtstr.c_str( ), value);
```
See also the data member function.

```
size_type capacity( ) const
```
Returns the number of characters allocated for use by this string. The string grows as needed; capacity tells you how much you can put in the string before it must grow again.

```
int compare(const basic_string& str) const
```
Compares two strings and returns:

< 0 if this string is less than str

= 0 if this string equals str

> 0 if this string is greater than str

```
int compare(size_type pos1, size_type n1,
            const basic_string& str) const
```
Constructs a temporary string *tmp*(*this, pos1, n1), and returns *tmp*.compare(str).

```
int compare(const charT* s) const
```
Constructs a temporary string *tmp*(s), and returns this->compare(*tmp*).

```
int compare(size_type pos1, size_type n1,const
            basic_string& str, size_type pos2, size_type
            n2) const
int compare(size_type pos1, size_type n1, const charT* s)
            const
int compare(size_type pos1, size_type n1, const charT* s,
            size_type n2) const
```
Constructs two temporary strings: *tmp1*(*this, pos1, n1) and *tmp2*: *tmp2*(str, pos2, n2), *tmp2*(s), or *tmp2*(s, n2). The function returns *tmp1*.compare(*tmp2*).

```
size_type copy(charT* dst, size_type n, size_type pos = 0)
               const
```
Copies up to n characters from this string, starting at position pos, to the character array dst. If pos > size(), out_of_range is thrown. The number of characters copied, *len*, is the smaller of n and size() - pos. The return value is *len*.

```
const charT* data() const
```
Returns a pointer to a character array that has the same character contents as this string. Note that the character array is not null-terminated. If size() == 0, data returns a valid, non-null pointer. You should not modify the contents of the data string. The pointer becomes invalid after calling any non-const member function of the string. See also the c_str member function.

```
basic_string& erase(size_type pos = 0, size_type n = npos)
```
Erases characters from this string, starting at position pos and erasing n or size( ) - pos characters, whichever is smaller. If pos > size( ), out_of_range is thrown. The return value is *this. For example:

```
std::string s("hello, world");
s.erase(9, 1) == "hello, wold"
s.erase(5)    == "hello"
```

```
size_type find(const basic_string& str, size_type pos = 0)
                 const
size_type find(const charT* s, size_type pos, size_type n)
                 const
size_type find(const charT* s, size_type pos = 0) const
size_type find(charT c, size_type pos = 0) const
```
Returns the smallest index of a substring or character, or npos if not found. The search starts at position pos. The string to search for is str or a temporary string *tmp* constructed as *tmp*(s, n), *tmp*(s), or *tmp*(1, c). In other words, find returns the smallest i such that $i >= pos$ and $i + str.size( ) <= size( )$ and $at(i+j) == str.at(j)$ for all j in $[0, str.size( ))$. For example:

```
std::string s("hello");
s.find('l')    == 2
s.find("lo", 2) == 3
s.find("low")  == string::npos
```

See also rfind, later in this section.

```
size_type find_first_not_of(const basic_string& str,
                             size_type pos = 0) const
```
Finds the first character at or after position pos that does not appear in str, or npos if every character appears in str. For example:

```
std::string s("hello");
s.find_first_not_of("aeiou")    == 0
s.find_first_not_of("aeiou", 1) == 2
s.find_first_not_of("aeiou", 6) == string::npos
```

```
size_type find_first_not_of(charT c, size_type pos = 0)
                                const
size_type find_first_not_of(const charT* s,
                                size_type pos = 0) const
size_type find_first_not_of(const charT* s, size_type pos,
                                size_type n) const
```

Constructs a temporary string *tmp* and returns find_first_not_of(*tmp*, pos), where *tmp* is constructed as *tmp*(1, c), *tmp*(s), or *tmp*(s, n).

```
size_type find_first_of(const basic_string& str,
                            size_type pos = 0) const
```

Returns the index of the first character at or after position pos that appears in str, or npos if no such character appears in str. For example:

```
std::string s("hello");
s.find_first_of("aeiou")    = 1
s.find_first_of("aeiou", 2) = 4
s.find_first_of("aeiou", 6) = string::npos
```

```
size_type find_first_of(charT c, size_type pos = 0) const
size_type find_first_of(const charT* s, size_type pos = 0)
                            const
size_type find_first_of(const charT* s, size_type pos,
                            size_type n) const
```

Constructs a temporary string *tmp* and returns find_first_of(*tmp*, pos), where *tmp* is constructed as *tmp*(1, c), *tmp*(s), or *tmp*(s, n).

```
size_type find_last_not_of(const basic_string& str,
                            size_type pos = npos) const
```

Returns the index of the last character at or before position pos that does not appear in str, or npos if every character appears in str. For example:

```
std::string s("hello");
s.find_last_not_of("aeiou")    == 3
s.find_last_not_of("aeiou", 1) == 0
s.find_last_not_of("aeiou", 0) == 0
```

```
size_type find_last_not_of(charT c, size_type pos = npos)
                              const
size_type find_last_not_of(const charT* s,size_type
                              pos = npos) const
size_type find_last_not_of(const charT* s,size_type
                              pos, size_type n) const
```
Constructs a temporary string *tmp* and returns find_last_
not_of(*tmp*, pos), where *tmp* is constructed as *tmp*(1, c),
tmp(s), or *tmp*(s, n).

```
size_type find_last_of(const basic_string& str,
                          size_type pos = npos) const
```
Returns the index of the last character at or before position pos that appears in str, or npos if no such character appears in str. For example:

```
std::string s("hello");
s.find_last_of("aeiou")    == 4
s.find_last_of("aeiou", 3) == 1
s.find_last_of("aeiou", 0) == string::npos
```

```
size_type find_last_of(charT c, size_type pos = npos) const
size_type find_last_of(const charT* s,
                          size_type pos = npos) const
size_type find_last_of(const charT* s, size_type pos,
                          size_type n) const
```
Constructs a temporary string *tmp* and returns find_last_
of(*tmp*, pos), where *tmp* is constructed as *tmp*(1, c),
tmp(s), or *tmp*(s, n).

```
basic_string& insert(size_type pos1,const basic_string&
                        str, size_type pos2, size_type n)
```
Inserts a substring of str into this string starting at position pos1. The substring to insert starts at pos2 and extends for up to n characters. If pos1 > size( ) or pos2 > str.size( ), out_of_range is thrown. The number of characters inserted is the smaller of n and str.size( ) - pos2. The return value is *this. For example:

```
std::string s("hi");
s.insert(2, ", world")        // s == "hi, world"
s.insert(2, "out there", 3, 42)// s == "hi there, world"
```

```
basic_string& insert(size_type pos, const
                     basic_string& str)
basic_string& insert(size_type pos, const charT* s,
                     size_type n)
basic_string& insert(size_type pos, const charT* s)
basic_string& insert(size_type pos, size_type n, charT c)
```
Returns insert(pos, str, 0, npos) or insert(pos, *tmp*, 0, npos), where the last three versions construct the temporary string *tmp* as *tmp*(s, n), *tmp*(s), or *tmp*(n, c).

```
size_type length( ) const
```
Returns size( ).

```
reference operator[](size_type n)
const_reference operator[](size_type n) const
```
Returns the character at index n, or charT( ) (the null character) if n == size( ). Behavior is undefined if n > size( ).

```
basic_string& operator=(const charT* s)
basic_string& operator=(charT c)
```
Constructs a temporary string, *tmp*(s) or *tmp*(1, c), and assigns *this = *tmp*. The return value is *this.

```
basic_string& operator+=(const basic_string& str)
basic_string& operator+=(const charT* s)
basic_string& operator+=(charT c)
```
Calls append with the same arguments and returns *this.

```
void push_back(charT c)
```
Appends c to the end of this string. The function's existence lets you use basic_string with a back_insert_iterator. Note that back and pop_back are not defined.

```
basic_string& replace(size_type pos1, size_type n1, const
                      basic_string& str, size_type pos2,
                      size_type n2)
```
Erases a substring and inserts another string in its place. The string to erase starts at pos1 and extends for up to n1 characters (or size( ) - pos1, whichever is smaller). The

string to insert is a substring of str, starting at pos2 and extending for up to n2 characters (or str.size( ) - pos2, whichever is smaller). The replacement string is inserted at pos1. If pos1 > size( ) or pos2 > str.size( ), out_of_range is thrown. The return value is *this.

```
std::string s("hello");
s.replace(1, 4, "appy")              s=="happy"
s.replace(5, 0, "your bday !", 4, 5) s=="happy bday"
s.replace(1, 1, 1, 'i')              s=="hippy bday"
```

basic_string& **replace**(size_type pos, size_type n1, const basic_string& str)

basic_string& **replace**(size_type pos, size_type n1, const charT* str)

basic_string& **replace**(size_type pos, size_type n1, const charT* s, size_type n2)

basic_string& **replace**(size_type pos, size_type n1, size_type n2, charT c)

Returns replace(pos, n1, tmp, 0, npos), where tmp is a temporary string constructed as tmp(str), tmp(s, n2), or tmp(n2, c).

basic_string& **replace**(iterator first, iterator last, const basic_string& str)

Erases the text in the range [first, last) and inserts str at the position where first pointed. The return value is *this.

basic_string& **replace**(iterator first, iterator last, const charT* s, size_type n)

basic_string& **replace**(iterator first, iterator last, const charT* s)

basic_string& **replace**(iterator first, iterator last, size_type n, charT c)

template<class InputIterator>
basic_string& **replace**(iterator first, iterator last, InputIterator i1, InputIterator i2)

Returns replace(first, last, tmp), in which tmp is a temporary string constructed as tmp(s, n), tmp(s), tmp(n, c), or tmp(i1, i2).

---

void **reserve**(size_type n = 0)

> Ensures that capacity( ) is at least as large as n. Call reserve to avoid the need to reallocate the string data repeatedly when you know the string will grow by small increments to a large size. Note that size( ) does not change.

void **resize**(size_type n, charT c)
void **resize**(size_type n)

> Changes the size of this string to n characters. If n <= size( ), the new string has the first n characters of the original string. If n > size( ), the new string has n - size( ) copies of c appended to the end. The second version returns resize(n, charT( )).

size_type **rfind**(const basic_string& str,
                    size_type pos = npos) const
size_type **rfind**(const charT* s, size_type pos,size_type n)
                    const
size_type **rfind**(const charT* s, size_type pos = npos) const
size_type **rfind**(charT c, size_type pos = npos) const

> Returns the largest index at or before pos of a substring or character, or npos if not found. The substring to search for is str or a temporary string *tmp* constructed as *tmp*(s, n), *tmp*(s), or *tmp*(1, c). In other words, rfind returns the largest i such that i <= pos and i + str.size( ) <= size( ) and at(i+j) == str.at(j) for all j in [0, str.size( )).
>
> See also find, earlier in this section. For example:

```
std::string s("hello");
s.rfind('l')    == 3
s.rfind("lo", 2) == string::npos
s.rfind("low")   == string::npos
```

basic_string **substr**(size_type pos = 0, size_type n = npos)
                    const

> Returns a substring that starts at position pos and extends for up to n characters (the smaller of n and size( ) - pos). If pos > size( ), out_of_range is thrown.

Vectors

A vector is a sequence container that has amortized constant performance for inserting and erasing at the end, and linear performance for inserting and erasing at any other point in the container. A vector supports random access iterators.

The vector class template is a standard sequence container that is like an array whose size can change at runtime. Elements of a vector are stored contiguously, just like an ordinary array. For most cases where you need an array, you should use a vector instead because a vector offers greater safety (no need for dynamic memory and raw pointers, the at member function checks array bounds, etc.).

All iterators, pointers, and references to a vector's elements become invalid when the vector's internal array is resized, which can happen for an insertion when the size matches the capacity, or when you explicitly change the size (e.g., by calling resize). You can ensure that an insertion does not force a resize by calling reserve to set the capacity prior to inserting one or more items. Iterators, pointers, and references also become invalid when they are past the point (at a higher index) where an item is inserted or erased.

NOTE

The standard library specializes vector<bool> to pack multiple bool values into an array of integers. The result is not a valid standard container because you cannot obtain a pointer to individual bool elements in the container. If you need a vector of bool values, use deque<bool> instead. For a fixed-size set of bits, use bitset.

The vector<T, Allocator> class template supports all the standard members for a sequence container, plus the following:

explicit **vector**(size_type n)
> Constructs a vector that contains n copies of T( ). Complexity is linear.

---

size_type **capacity**( ) const

>   Returns the maximum number of items that can be stored in the vector before it must be resized. Complexity is constant.

void **reserve**(size_type n)

>   Ensures that capacity( ) is at least n. Call reserve to avoid the need to reallocate the vector repeatedly when you know the vector will grow by small increments to a large size, or when you want to ensure iterators do not become invalid after inserting one or more items. Note that size( ) does not change. Complexity is linear.

void **resize**(size_type sz, T t = T( ))

>   Changes the size of this vector to n. If n > size( ), one or more copies of t are added to the end of the vector to reach the desired size. If the new size is smaller than the current size, elements are erased from the end to reach the new size. Complexity is linear.

The vector class template implements the following optional member functions:

at	operator[]
back	pop_back
front	push_back

Iterators

An iterator is an abstraction of a pointer used for pointing into containers and other sequences. An ordinary pointer can point to various elements in an array or to one position past the last element of an array. The ++ operator advances the pointer to the next element, and the * operator dereferences the pointer to return a value from the array. Iterators generalize the concept so the same operators have the same behavior for any container, even trees and lists.

You can look at iterators from two different perspectives: the implementor's or the user's. This book does not cover the implementation of iterators. To use an iterator, you must know the iterator's category and traits. These topics are covered in this section, along with a number of specialized iterators. All function and class templates discussed in this section are declared in the <iterator> header.

Iterator Categories

There are five categories of iterators:

Input
> Lets you read a sequence in one pass. The increment operator (++) advances to the next element, but there is no decrement operator. Use the dereference operator (*) to read elements. You cannot read a single element more than once, and you cannot modify elements.

Output
> Lets you write a sequence in one pass. The increment operator (++) advances to the next element, but there is no decrement operator. Use the dereference operator (*) only to assign a value to an element. You cannot assign a value more than once to a single element. Unlike other iterator categories, you cannot compare output iterators.

Forward
> Permits unidirectional access to a sequence. Use the increment operator (++) to advance the iterator and the dereference operator (*) to read or write an element. You can refer to and assign to an item as many times as you want. You can use a forward iterator anywhere an input or output iterator is required.

Bidirectional
> Similar to a forward iterator, but it also supports the decrement operator (--) to move the iterator backward by one position.

Random access

Similar to a bidirectional iterator, but it also supports the [] (subscript) operator to access any index in the sequence. Also, you can add or subtract an integer to move a random access iterator by more than one position at a time. Subtracting two random access iterators yields an integer distance between them. Thus, a random access iterator is most like a conventional pointer, and a pointer can be used as a random access iterator.

An input, forward, bidirectional, or random access iterator can be a const_iterator. Dereferencing a const_iterator yields a constant value; otherwise, it behaves as described above. See "const_iterators" later in this section for details.

Using Iterators

The most important point to remember about iterators is that they are potentially unsafe. Like pointers, an iterator can point to a container that has been destroyed or to an element that has been erased. You can advance an iterator past the end of the container in the same way a pointer can point past the end of an array. With a little care and caution, however, iterators are safe to use.

The first key to safe use of iterators is to make sure a program never dereferences an iterator that marks the end of a range. A typical usage of iterators is to denote a range of values, such as the contents of a container. One iterator points to the start of the range, and another marks the end of the range by pointing to a position one past the last element in the range. The mathematical notation of [first, last) tells you that the item that first points to is included in the range, but that the item that last points to is excluded from the range.

Even a valid iterator can become invalid and therefore unsafe to use. For example, a valid iterator can become invalid if the item to which the iterator points is erased. In general, iterators for the node-based containers (list, set, multiset, map, multimap) become invalid only when they point to an erased node. Iterators for the array-based containers (basic_string, deque, vector) become invalid when the underlying array is reallocated, which might happen for any insertion and for some erasures.

An uninitialized iterator is unsafe, just as an uninitialized pointer is unsafe to dereference. Typically, a valid iterator is obtained by calling a container's begin() or end() member function, or by constructing a special iterator such as istream_iterator, or an iterator adapter such as reverse_ iterator.

For example, to copy one list to another (assuming the desti- nation list has enough room), do the following:

```
std::copy(src_list.begin(), src_list.end(),
          dst_list.begin());
```

You can also use ordinary pointers as iterators. For example, to copy the contents of an array into a vector:

```
static const std::size_t num_data = 4;
int data[num_data] = { 10, 20, 30, 42 };
std::vector<int> vecdata;
std::copy(data, data + num_data,
          std::back_inserter(vecdata));
```

Notice how the end of the range is computed as an offset from the start of the range. You must be sure to specify the correct end of the range. A common idiom is to use sizeof to count the number of items in an array:

```
int data[] = { 10, 20, 30, 42 };
std::vector<int> vecdata;
std::copy(data, data + sizeof(data)/sizeof(*data),
          std::back_inserter(vecdata));
```

You can also use a function template and let the compiler deduce the array size for you. The only drawback of this approach is that the array size is not a compile-time con- stant, but in this case the limitation is irrelevant:

```
// Return the number of elements in an array.
template<typename T, std::size_t N>
inline std::size_t array_size(T (&)[N])
{
  return N;
}

int data[] = { 10, 20, 30, 42 };
std::vector<int> vecdata(array_size(data));
std::copy(data, data + array_size(data),
          vecdata.begin( ));
```

Iterator Traits

An iterator might be implemented as a pointer or as a class,
perhaps a class that derives from the standard iterator class
template. Any pointer can also be treated as an iterator. The
iterator_traits class template presents a common interface
to all kinds of iterators. All the members of iterator_traits
are typedef declarations:

iterator_category
> Must be one of the five iterator category tags:
>
>> bidirectional_iterator_tag
>> forward_iterator_tag
>> input_iterator_tag
>> output_iterator_tag
>> random_access_iterator_tag

value_type
> The element type. It can be void for an output iterator
> because you cannot dereference an output iterator.

difference_type
> An integral type that represents the distance between two
> iterators. It can be void for an output iterator because
> you cannot measure the distance between two output
> iterators. Many iterators use ptrdiff_t, which is suitable
> for typical pointer-like iterators.

pointer

> The pointer-to-element type. Most iterators use value_type*.

reference

> The reference-to-element type. Most iterators use value_type&.

The iterator_traits template is specialized for pointers (T*) and pointers to const (const T*). The value_type is the pointer's base type (T); the difference_type is ptrdiff_t; the pointer type is the same as the template parameter (T* or const T*); and the reference type is the reference equivalent of pointer (T& or const T&).

When you write code, such as a custom algorithm, you should use the iterator traits to ensure your code works with plain pointers as well as fancier iterators. For example, suppose you write a function to return the median of any range:

```
template<typename FwdIter, typename Compare>
FwdIter median(FwdIter first, FwdIter last, Compare comp)
{
  using namespace std;
  typedef typename iterator_traits<FwdIter>::value_type
    value_type;
  vector<value_type> tmp(first, last);
  typename vector<value_type>::size_type
    median_pos = tmp.size() / 2;
  nth_element(tmp.begin(), tmp.begin() + median_pos,
              tmp.end(), comp);
  return find(first, last, tmp[median_pos]);
}
```

If you use an iterator object for the first and last arguments (say, from a container's begin() and end() functions), the iterator_traits template obtains its value_type from the iterator class's value_type member. If you use plain pointers, the iterator_traits template specialization extracts the pointer's base type as value_type.

---

const_iterators

Every container must provide an `iterator` type and a `const_iterator` type. Functions such as `begin()` and `end()` return `iterator` when called on a non-const container and return `const_iterator` when called on a const container.

Note that a `const_iterator` (with underscore) is different from a `const iterator` (without underscore). A `const iterator` is a constant object of type `iterator`. Being constant, it cannot change, so it cannot advance to point to a different position. A `const_iterator`, on the other hand, is a non-const object of type `const_iterator`. It is not constant, so it can change value. The key difference between `iterator` and `const_iterator` is that `iterator` returns lvalues of type `T`, and `const_iterator` returns unmodifiable objects, either rvalues or const lvalues of type `T`. The standard requires that a plain iterator be convertible to `const_iterator`, but not the other way around.

One problem is that some members of the standard containers (most notably erase and insert) take `iterator` (that is, the container's `iterator` type member, not the standard iterator class template) as parameters, not `const_iterator`. If you have a `const_iterator`, you cannot use it as an insertion or erasure position.

Another problem is that it might be difficult to compare an iterator with a `const_iterator`. If the compiler reports an error when you try to compare iterators for equality or inequality, try swapping the order of the iterators. For example, if `x == y` fails to compile, try `y == x`. The problem, most likely, is that `y` is a `const_iterator` and `x` is a plain `iterator`. By swapping the order, you let the compiler convert `x` to a `const_iterator` and allow the comparison.

Insertion Iterators

An insertion iterator is a kind of output iterator that inserts items into a container. The insertion iterators all work in a similar fashion. The increment operator (++) is a no-op (it does nothing), and the iterator does not actually keep track of any position. The dereference operator (*) returns the iterator, not a value. The assignment operator (=) is then overloaded to insert the right-hand operand in the container:

```
vector<int> data;
back_insert_iterator<vector<int> > iter(data);
*data = 10;
*data = 20;
*data = 30;
// data now contains { 10, 20, 30 }
```

This implementation of an iterator seems odd, but it meets the criteria of an output iterator. When you use it as an ordinary output iterator, it works just the way you want it to work.

For your convenience, each insertion iterator has a companion function template that constructs an iterator object. The function template uses argument type deduction to spare you the effort of specifying the container type explicitly.

The three insertion iterator function templates are:

```
template <typename Container>
back_insert_iterator<Container>
```
back_inserter(Container& x)

> Constructs a back_insert_iterator to insert items at the end of the container x by calling push_back. The compiler can deduce the Container type, which can be basic_string, deque, list, vector, or a custom container type that has a push_back member function.

```
template <typename Container>
front_insert_iterator<Container>
```
front_inserter(Container& x)

> Constructs a front_insert_iterator object to insert items at the start of the container x by calling push_front.

The compiler can deduce the Container type, which can be deque, list, or a custom container type that has a push_front member function.

```
template <typename Container, typename Iterator>
insert_iterator<Container>
inserter(Container& x, Iterator pos)
```
Constructs an insert_iterator object to insert items in the container x. If x is a sequence container, new items are inserted immediately before position pos. If x is an associative container, items are inserted at the appropriate positions, and the complexity is logarithmic for each insertion.

The compiler deduces the Container type, which can be any standard-conformant container type (with the insert(iterator, const value_type&) member).

I/O Stream Iterators

The <iterator> header declares four iterators that perform I/O. Two are input iterators, and two are output iterators. Two work with stream buffers, and two work with streams. The stream buffer iterators read and write characters (narrow or wide), and the stream iterators read and write sequences of a value type that supports operator>> for input or operator<< for output.

istream_iterator class template

The istream_iterator<T, CharT, Traits, Distance> class template wraps an input iterator around an input stream (an instance of basic_istream), making the stream appear to be a sequence of items, each of type T. The following are the members of istream_iterator:

char_type
    The stream's character type (a synonym for the CharT template parameter; the default is char).

istream_type

A synonym for the stream type, that is, basic_istream<CharT, Traits>.

traits_type

The stream's character traits type (a synonym for the Traits template parameter; the default is std::char_traits<CharT>, which is declared in <string>).

istream_iterator( )

Constructs an istream_iterator that denotes the end of the stream. End-of-stream iterators are equal to each other and are not equal to any other istream_iterator.

istream_iterator(istream_type& stream)

Constructs an istream_iterator to read from stream. The constructor might read the first item from the stream. An istream_iterator that wraps a stream is equal to an end-of-stream iterator when stream.eof( ) returns true.

istream_iterator(const istream_iterator<T,CharT,Traits, Distance>& iter)

Constructs a copy of iter. Note that two istream_iterator objects are the same (operator== returns true) if they point to the same stream object.

const T& **operator*( )** const

Returns the item that was read most recently from the stream.

const T* **operator->( )**

Returns a pointer to the item that was read most recently from the stream.

const istream_iterator<T,CharT,Traits,Distance>&
operator++( )

Reads the next item from the stream using operator>>. The return value is *this.

```
istream_iterator<T,CharT,Traits,Distance>
operator++(int)
```
> Reads the next item from the stream using operator>>.
> The return value is a copy of *this, made prior to read-
> ing from the stream.

istreambuf_iterator class template

The istreambuf_iterator<CharT, Traits> class template
wraps a stream buffer object (instance of basic_streambuf) as
an input iterator to read characters from the stream buffer.

The post-increment operator (++) returns a *proxy object*,
which is an object that stands in for the istreambuf_iterator
object. Its use is largely transparent, and you rarely need to
think about it. The definition and name of the proxy class are
implementation-defined, but the class has at least the capa-
bility to return the underlying stream buffer and a character
that was read from the stream buffer. This section assumes
the class name is *proxy*. Example 1 shows a prototypical
implementation of *proxy*.

Example 1. A trivial implementation of the proxy class

```
template<typename CharT,
         typename Traits=char_traits<CharT> >
class istreambuf_iterator<CharT, Traits>::proxy
{
  friend template<typename CharT, typename Traits>
    class istreambuf_iterator<CharT,Traits>;
public:
  CharT operator*() { return keep; }
private:
  CharT keep;
  basic_streambuf<CharT,Traits>* sbuf;
  proxy(CharT c, basic_streambuf<CharT,Traits>* sbuf);
    : keep(c), sbuf(sbuf) {}
};
```

In the following descriptions of the member functions of istreambuf_iterator, the data member *sbuf* is a pointer to the iterator's stream buffer. The *sbuf* member serves only to keep the function descriptions clear and simple; the class is not required to have such a member, nor is the class required to have a member with that name.

char_type
> The stream's character type (a synonym for the CharT template parameter).

int_type
> A synonym for the character traits' int_type.

istream_type
> A synonym for the stream type, that is, basic_istream<CharT, Traits>.

streambuf_type
> A synonym for the stream buffer type, that is, basic_streambuf<CharT, Traits>.

traits_type
> The stream's character traits type (a synonym for the Traits template parameter).

istreambuf_iterator( ) throw( )
> Constructs the end-of-stream iterator.

istreambuf_iterator(istream_type& s) throw( )
istreambuf_iterator(streambuf_type* sb) throw( )
istreambuf_iterator(const *proxy*& p) throw( )
> Constructs an istreambuf_iterator and initializes *sbuf* to s.rdbuf( ), sb, or p.sbuf. If sb == 0, an end-of-stream iterator is constructed.

CharT **operator***( ) const
> Returns the next character by calling *sbuf*->sgetc( ).

istreambuf_iterator<charT,traits>& **operator++**( )
> Calls *sbuf*->sbumpc( ) to read the next character, and returns *this.

proxy **operator++**(int)
> Returns *proxy(sbuf->sbumpc( ), sbuf)*.

bool **equal**(istreambuf_iterator& b) const
> Returns true if both iterators are end-of-stream iterators or if neither iterator is an end-of-stream iterator. The iterators do not have to use the same stream buffer.

ostream_iterator class template

The ostream_iterator<T, CharT, Traits, Distance> class template wraps an output iterator around an output stream (instance of basic_ostream), making the stream appear to be a sequence of items, each of type T. The following are the members of ostream_iterator:

char_type
> The stream's character type (a synonym for the CharT template parameter; the default is char).

istream_type
> A synonym for the stream type, that is, basic_ostream<CharT, Traits>.

traits_type
> The stream's character traits type (a synonym for the Traits template parameter; the default is std::char_traits<CharT>, which is declared in <string>).

ostream_iterator(ostream_type& stream)
ostream_iterator(ostream_type& stream, const CharT* delim)
ostream_iterator(const ostream_iterator<T,CharT, Traits>& x)
> Prepares to write items to stream. If delim is present, it will be written after each item. The copy constructor copies the reference to the stream and to the delimiter from x.

```
ostream_iterator<T,charT,traits>&
```
operator=(const T& value)
> Writes value to the stream using operator<<. If the ostream_iterator has a delimiter, it is written after value. The return value is *this.

```
ostream_iterator<T,charT,traits>& operator*( )
```
> Returns *this.

```
ostream_iterator<T,charT,traits>& operator++( )
ostream_iterator<T,charT,traits>& operator++(int)
```
> Returns *this with no side effects.

ostreambuf_iterator class template

The ostreambuf_iterator<CharT, Traits> class template wraps a basic_streambuf object as an output iterator to write characters to the stream buffer.

In the following descriptions of the members of ostreambuf_iterator, the data member *sbuf* is a pointer to the iterator's stream buffer. The *sbuf* member serves only to keep the function descriptions clear and simple; the class is not required to have such a member, or a member with that name.

char_type
> The stream's character type (a synonym for the CharT template parameter).

ostream_type
> A synonym for the stream type, that is, basic_ostream<CharT, Traits>.

streambuf_type
> A synonym for the stream buffer type, that is, basic_streambuf<CharT, Traits>.

traits_type
> The stream's character traits type (a synonym for the Traits template parameter).

```
ostreambuf_iterator(ostream_type& s) throw( )
ostreambuf_iterator(streambuf_type* sb) throw( )
```
Saves the stream buffer s.rdbuf( ) or sb in *sbuf*.

```
ostreambuf_iterator& operator=(charT c)
```
Calls *sbuf*->sputc(c) to write the character c (only if failed( ) returns false), and returns *this.

```
ostreambuf_iterator& operator*( )
```
Returns *this.

```
ostreambuf_iterator& operator++( )
ostreambuf_iterator& operator++(int)
```
Returns *this.

```
bool failed( ) const throw( )
```
Returns true if *sbuf*->sputc( ) ever returned Traits:: eof( ). Otherwise, it returns false.

Raw Storage Iterator

The raw_storage_iterator<OutputIterator, T> class template implements an output iterator that writes to uninitialized memory. It is declared in the <memory> header. The first template parameter is the type of an output iterator to be adapted. The output iterator must have operator& that returns a pointer to T. For example, you can use a pointer to newly allocated, uninitialized memory as the output iterator.

Use the raw_storage_iterator as you would any other output iterator. The member functions are as follows:

```
explicit raw_storage_iterator(OutputIterator x)
```
Constructs a raw storage iterator that points to the same element as x.

```
raw_storage_iterator<OutputIterator,T>& operator*( )
```
Returns *this.

```
raw_storage_iterator<OutputIterator,T>&
```
operator=(const T& element)
>Constructs a copy of element in the raw storage where the iterator points.

```
raw_storage_iterator<OutputIterator,T>& operator++( )
```
>Advances the iterator and returns *this.

```
raw_storage_iterator<OutputIterator,T> operator++(int)
```
>Advances the iterator and returns a copy of *this made prior to advancement.

Reverse Iterators

Every container that supports bidirectional or random access iterators also provides reverse iterators, which start at the last element and "advance" toward the first element of the container. These iterators are named reverse_iterator and const_reverse_iterator.

The standard library includes the reverse_iterator class template as a convenient way to implement a container's reverse iterator types. The reverse_iterator class template is an iterator adapter that runs in the reverse direction of the adapted iterator. The adapted iterator must be a bidirectional or random access iterator. Given a reverse iterator, you can obtain the adapted iterator by calling the base( ) function.

On paper, the reverse iterator seems like a good idea. After all, a bidirectional iterator can run in two directions. There is no reason why an iterator adapter could not implement operator++ by calling the adapted iterator's operator-- function.

However, reverse iterators share a problem with const_ iterators, namely that several container members, such as insert and erase, require the container's exact iterator member type. The reverse_iterator type is not accepted, so you must pass the adapted iterator instead.

Because an iterator can point to one item past the last item in a container but cannot point to one item before the first, a reverse iterator conceptually points to one item *before* the position to which the adapted iterator points. This works fine as an insertion point, but for erasing, the reverse iterator is one off from the desired position. The solution is to increment the reverse iterator, call base( ) to obtain the adapted iterator, and then pass the adapted iterator to erase.

The following are the members of reverse_iterator:

current
> The adapted iterator. This data member is protected; see base( ) for read-only public access to the adapted iterator.

reverse_iterator( )
> Initializes the current data member with its default constructor.

explicit **reverse_iterator**(Iterator iter)
> Initializes the current data member to iter.

template <typename U>
reverse_iterator(const reverse_iterator<U>& ri)
> Initializes the current data member to ri.base( ).

Iterator **base**( ) const
> Returns the adapted iterator, current. Note that the adapted iterator points to one position *after* the reverse iterator's logical position.

reference **operator***( ) const
> Returns a reference to the item that the reverse iterator logically points to, which is one item *before* the item to which base( ) points. Thus, you can think of the dereference function working as follows:

```
reference operator*( ) const {
  iterator_type tmp = base( );
  --tmp;
  return *tmp;
}
```

```
pointer operator->( ) const
```
Returns a pointer to the item that the reverse iterator log-
ically points to, that is, &(operator*( )).

```
reverse_iterator& operator++( )
```
Decrements current and returns *this.

```
reverse_iterator operator++(int)
```
Saves a copy of *this, decrements current, and returns
the saved copy of *this.

```
reverse_iterator& operator--( )
```
Increments current and returns *this.

```
reverse_iterator operator--(int)
```
Saves a copy of *this, increments current, and returns
the saved copy of *this.

```
reverse_iterator operator+(difference_type n) const
```
Returns reverse_iterator(base( ) - n).

```
reverse_iterator& operator+=(difference_type n)
```
Subtracts n from current and returns *this.

```
reverse_iterator operator-(difference_type n) const
```
Returns reverse_iterator(base( ) + n).

```
reverse_iterator& operator-=(difference_type n)
```
Adds n to current and returns *this.

```
reference operator[](difference_type n) const
```
Returns base( )[-n-1].

Following are several non-member functions for comparing
reverse iterators and for performing basic arithmetic: finding
the distance between two reverse iterators and advancing a
reverse iterator by an integer.

```
template <typename Iterator>
bool operator==(const reverse_iterator<Iterator>& x,
                const reverse_iterator<Iterator>& y)
```
Returns true when the base iterators are equal, that is,
x.base( ) == y.base( ).

```
template <typename Iterator>
bool operator!=(const reverse_iterator<Iterator>& x,
                const reverse_iterator<Iterator>& y)
```
Returns true when x and y have different base iterators,
that is, x.base( ) != y.base( ).

```
template <typename Iterator>
bool operator<(const reverse_iterator<Iterator>& x,
               const reverse_iterator<Iterator>& y)
```
Returns true when x is closer than y to the beginning of
the sequence. Because x and y are reverse iterators, the
function returns y.base( ) < x.base( ).

```
template <typename Iterator>
bool operator>(const reverse_iterator<Iterator>& x,
               const reverse_iterator<Iterator>& y)
```
Returns true when x is farther than y from the beginning
of the sequence. Because x and y are reverse iterators, the
function returns y.base( ) > x.base( ).

```
template <typename Iterator>
bool operator>=(const reverse_iterator<Iterator>& x,
                const reverse_iterator<Iterator>& y)
```
Returns true when x is farther than y from the beginning
of the sequence or x equals y. Because x and y are reverse
iterators, the function returns y.base( ) >= x.base( ).

```
template <typename Iterator>
bool operator<=(const reverse_iterator<Iterator>& x,
                const reverse_iterator<Iterator>& y)
```
Returns true when x is closer than y to the beginning of
the sequence or x equals y. Because x and y are reverse
iterators, the function returns y.base( ) <= x.base( ).

```
template <typename Iterator>
typename reverse_iterator<Iterator>::difference_type
operator-(const reverse_iterator<Iterator>& x,
          const reverse_iterator<Iterator>& y)
```
Returns the distance between two reverse iterators, that
is, y.base( ) - x.base( ).

```
template <typename Iter>
reverse_iterator<Iter>
operator+(typename reverse_iterator<Iter>::
          difference_type n,const
          reverse_iterator<Iter>& ri)
```
Advances a reverse iterator ri by n. This function is a counterpart to the operator+ member function, allowing you to write ri + n and n + ri, which yield the same result.

Iterator Function Templates

The <iterator> header declares two function templates for working with iterators:

```
template <typename InputIterator, typename Distance>
void advance(InputIterator& iter, Distance n)
```
Advances an input iterator iter by the distance n. If the iterator is bidirectional or random access, n can be negative. If the iterator is random access, the advance function is specialized as iter + n; other iterators apply the ++ operator n times (or -- for a bidirectional iterator when n is negative).

```
template<typename InputIterator>
typename iterator_traits<InputIterator>::difference_type
distance(InputIterator first, InputIterator last)
```
Returns the number of elements between first and last. The function is specialized for random access iterators to return last - first; for other input iterators, the function applies the ++ operator to first until first == last. The behavior is undefined if first and last refer to different containers or if last points to an element earlier than first.

Algorithms

The so-called algorithms in the standard library distinguish C++ from other programming languages. Every major programming language has a suite of container types, but in the traditional object-oriented approach, each container class defines the operations that it permits, e.g., sorting, searching, and modifying. C++ turns object-oriented programming on its head and provides a set of function templates, called algorithms, that work with iterators, and therefore with almost any container.

Most of the standard algorithms are declared in the <algorithm> header, with some numerical algorithms in <numeric>, and a few algorithms in <memory> for working with uninitialized buffers. Unless otherwise mentioned, the function templates in this section are declared in <algorithm>. This section organizes the algorithms in groups of related functions. To find a specific algorithm by name, check the index.

The type of every function parameter in this section is a type template parameter. For the sake of brevity, the template header is omitted from each declaration. The compiler usually deduces the template parameter types. If you must specify an explicit template argument, the order of the template parameters matches the order of their use in the function parameters.

The names of the template parameters tell you what kind of template argument is expected, especially the iterator category. The iterator category is the minimal functionality needed, so you can, for example, use a random access iterator where at least a forward iterator is needed. To keep the syntax summaries short and readable, the iterator categories are abbreviated, as shown in Table 1.

Table 1. Template parameter names for iterator categories

Parameter name	Iterator category
BiDi	Bidirectional iterator
Fwd	Forward iterator
Inp	Input iterator
Out	Output iterator
Rnd	Random access iterator

A number of algorithms require sorted ranges or otherwise use a comparison function to test the less-than relationship. The library overloads each algorithm: the first function uses operator< and the second accepts a function pointer or function object to perform the comparison. The comparison function takes two arguments and returns a Boolean result (type bool or implicitly convertible to bool). If you overload operator< or provide your own comparison function, make sure it correctly implements a less-than relationship. In particular, A < A must be false for any A, and if A < B and B < C, then A < C.

In this section, the following conventions are used:

- Iterators are usually used in ranges that represent all the elements in the range or sequence. A range is written using standard mathematical notation: a square bracket denotes an inclusive endpoint of a range, and a parenthesis denotes an exclusive endpoint of a range. Thus, [x, y) signifies a range that starts at x, including x, and ends at y, excluding y.

- The names used for input ranges are typically first and last, where first is an iterator that points to the first element of a range, and last is an iterator that points to one past the end of the range. Thus, the range is written as [first, last).

- An iterator that advances from first to last is typically called iter.

- Output iterators are typically named result. Most algorithms require only the start of the output range. It is your responsibility to ensure the output range has room to accommodate the entire output. The behavior is undefined if the output range overflows.

- A *functor* or *function object* is an object that has an overloaded operator( ). See the later section, "Function Objects," for more information.

- A *predicate* is a function or functor that returns a Boolean result, that is, a result that can be implicitly converted to bool.

Nonmodifying Operations

These algorithms examine every element of a sequence without modifying the order.

```
typename iterator_traits<Inp>::difference_type
count(Inp first, Inp last, const T& val)
```
Returns the number of times val occurs in the range [first, last). Items are compared with the == operator. See also the count member function for associative containers.

```
typename iterator_traits<Inp>::difference_type
count_if(Inp first, Inp last, Pred pred)
```
Returns the number of times pred returns true when called for items in the range [first, last).

```
Function for_each(Inp first, Inp last, Func func)
```
Calls func for each item in the range [first, last) and returns a copy of func.

Comparison

These algorithms compare objects or sequences (without modifying the elements).

```
bool equal(Inp1 first1, Inp1 last1, Inp2 first2)
bool equal(Inp1 first1, Inp1 last1, Inp2 first2,
           BinPred pred)
```
Tests whether two ranges have equivalent contents. Items in the range [first, last) are compared with items in the range that starts at first2 and has the same number of elements as the first range. The first form of equal compares items with the == operator; the second form calls pred(*iter1, *iter2).

```
bool lexicographical_compare(Inp1 first1, Inp1 last1,
                             Inp2 first2, Inp2 last2)
bool lexicographical_compare(Inp1 first1, Inp1 last1,
                             Inp2 first2, Inp2 last2,
                             Cmp comp)
```
Determines whether the range [first1, last1) is less than the range [first2, last2). Items are compared element-wise until a pair of elements *iter1 and *iter2 are different or one range ends.

The return value is true if the first range is "less than" the second. If comparison stops because a pair of elements differs, the return value is true if *iter1 is less than *iter2. If the first range is a subsequence of the second, true is returned. Otherwise, false is returned.

The first form compares elements with the < operator. The second form calls comp(*iter1, *iter2).

```
const T& max(const T& a, const T& b)
const T& max(const T& a, const T& b, Cmp comp)
```
Returns the maximum of two values a and b. The first form compares the values with the < operator. The second form calls comp.

```
Fwd max_element(Fwd first, Fwd last)
Fwd max_element(Fwd first, Fwd last, Cmp comp)
```
Returns an iterator that points to the first occurrence of the largest element in the range [first, last). If the

range is empty, last is returned. The first form compares values with the < operator. The second form calls comp.

```
const T& min(const T& a, const T& b)
const T& min(const T& a, const T& b, Cmp comp)
```
Returns the minimum of two values a and b. The first form compares the values with the < operator. The second form calls comp.

```
Fwd min_element(Fwd first, Fwd last)
Fwd min_element(Fwd first, Fwd last, Cmp comp)
```
Returns an iterator that points to the first occurrence of the smallest element in the range [first, last). If the range is empty, last is returned. The first form compares values with the < operator. The second form calls comp.

```
pair<Inp1, Inp2>
mismatch(Inp1 first1, Inp1 last1, Inp2 first2)
pair<Inp1, Inp2>
mismatch(Inp1 first1, Inp1 last1, Inp2 first2,
        BinPred pred)
```
Finds the first position where two ranges differ. The return value is a pair of *iter1* and *iter2*, where *iter1* is in the range [first1, last1), and *iter2* is in the range that starts at *iter2* and has the same length as the first range. The values of *iter1* and *iter2* are the smallest (closest to first1 and first2) positions where *iter1* is not equal to *iter2*.

The first form compares elements with the == operator. The second form returns the pair of positions where pred(*iter1*, *iter2*) returns false.

Searching

These algorithms search for a value or a subsequence in a sequence (without modifying the elements).

```
Fwd adjacent_find(Fwd first, Fwd last)
Fwd adjacent_find(Fwd first, Fwd last, BinPred pred)
```
Finds the first position in [first, last) where an item (*iter*) is equal to its neighbor (*(iter+1)*). The first form compares items with the == operator. The second form calls pred. If no neighbors are equal, last is returned.

```
Inp find(Inp first, Inp last, const T& value)
```
Finds the first occurrence of value in the range [first, last) and returns an iterator that points to the value. If value is not found, last is returned.

```
Fwd1 find_end(Fwd1 first1, Fwd1 last1,
              Fwd2 first2, Fwd2 last2)
Fwd1 find_end(Fwd1 first1, Fwd1 last1,
              Fwd2 first2, Fwd2 last2, BinPred pred)
```
Finds the last occurrence of a subsequence [first2, last2) in the range [first1, last1). If the subsequence is not found, last1 is returned.

```
Fwd1 find_first_of(Fwd1 first1, Fwd1 last1,
                   Fwd2 first2, Fwd2 last2)
Fwd1 find_first_of(Fwd1 first1, Fwd1 last1,
                   Fwd2 first2, Fwd2 last2, BinPred pred)
```
Finds the first position in the range [first1, last1) where a value matches any one item from the range [first2, last2). The first form compares items with the == operator. The second form calls pred. If no value from the second range is found in the first range, last1 is returned.

```
Inp find_if(Inp first, Inp last, Pred pred)
```
Finds the first item in [first, last) for which pred returns true, and returns an iterator that points to that item. If pred always returns false, last is returned.

```
Fwd1 search(Fwd1 first1, Fwd1 last1, Fwd2 first2,
           Fwd2 last2)
Fwd1 search(Fwd1 first1, Fwd1 last1,
           Fwd2 first2, Fwd2 last2, BinPred pred)
```
Finds a subsequence [first2, last2) in a range [first1, last1) and returns an iterator that points to the first occurrence of the subsequence. If the subsequence is not found, last1 is returned.

```
Fwd search_n(Fwd first, Fwd last, Size count,
            const T& value)
Fwd search_n(Fwd first, Fwd last, Size count,
            const T& value, BinPred pred)
```
Finds a subsequence (count occurrences of value) in a range [first, last) and returns an iterator that points to the first occurrence of the subsequence. If the subsequence is not found, last is returned.

Binary Search

These algorithms perform a binary search on a sorted sequence. The range must be sorted in ascending order using the < operator or a caller-supplied comparison function. The sequence typically comes from a sequence container for which you have already sorted the elements. You can use an associative container, but you will get better performance by calling one of the member functions with the same name (i.e., equal_range, lower_bound, upper_bound).

```
bool binary_search(Fwd first, Fwd last, const T& value)
bool binary_search(Fwd first, Fwd last, const T& value,
                  Cmp comp)
```
Searches for value in the range [first, last). The items must be sorted in ascending order using the < operator (first form) or comp (second form). The return value is true if value is found or false if not found.

```
pair<Fwd, Fwd>
equal_range(Fwd first, Fwd last, const T& value)
pair<Fwd, Fwd>
equal_range(Fwd first, Fwd last, const T& value,
            Cmp comp)
```
Finds the upper and lower bounds of value's position in
the sorted range [first, last). If value is not in the range,
both elements of the pair are equal, pointing to the position where value belongs in the range. If value occurs
one or more times, the first member of the returned
pair points to the first occurrence of value, and the
second member points to one past the last occurrence.
Thus, the return value is equivalent to the following:

```
make_pair(lower_bound(first, last, value),
          upper_bound(first, last, value))
```

```
Fwd lower_bound(Fwd first, Fwd last, const T& value)
Fwd lower_bound(Fwd first, Fwd last, const T& value,
                Cmp comp)
```
Finds the lower bound for value's position in the sorted
range [first, last). The return value is an iterator that
points to the first occurrence of value if it is in the range;
otherwise, the iterator points to the position of the first
item greater than value.

```
Fwd upper_bound(Fwd first, Fwd last, const T& value)
Fwd upper_bound(Fwd first, Fwd last, const T& value,
                Cmp comp)
```
Finds the upper bound for value's position in the sorted
range [first, last). The return value is an iterator that
points to the position of the first item greater than value.

Modifying Sequence Operations

These algorithms modify a sequence:

```
Out copy(Inp first, Inp last, Out result)
```
Copies every item in the range [first, last) to the range
that starts at result. You must ensure the output range
has enough room for the entire copy.

```
BiDi2 copy_backward(BiDi1 first, BiDi1 last,
                    BiDi2 result)
```
Copies a range [first, last) to the output range that ends at one position before result. Thus, *first is copied to *--result, and result is repeatedly decremented and assigned to until the input reaches last (which is not copied). You must ensure that the output range has enough room for the entire copy.

```
void fill(Fwd first, Fwd last, const T& value)
```
Fills the range [first, last) with copies of value.

```
void fill_n(Out first, Size n, const T& value)
```
Fills the range [first, first+n) with copies of value.

```
void generate(Fwd first, Fwd last, Gen gen)
```
Fills the range [first, last) with the values returned from repeated calls to gen( ).

```
void generate_n(Out first, Size n, Gen gen)
```
Fills the range [first, first+n) with the values returned from repeated calls to gen( ).

```
void iter_swap(Fwd1 a, Fwd2 b)
```
Swaps the values *a and *b. See also swap.

```
void random_shuffle(Rnd first, Rnd last)
void random_shuffle(Rnd first, Rnd last,
                    RandomNumberGenerator& rand)
```
Reorders the range [first, last) into a random order. The first form calls an implementation-defined random number generator; the second form repeatedly calls rand(n) to generate a pseudo-random number in the range [0, n).

```
Fwd remove(Fwd first, Fwd last, const T& value)
```
Reorders the range [first, last) to prepare for erasing all elements equal to value. The return value is an iterator such that all elements in the range [first, *return*) are not equal to value. Typical usage of remove is to erase the

removed elements by calling a container's erase(*return*, last) member function, passing remove's return value as the first argument to erase.

Out **remove_copy**(Inp first, Inp last, Out result,
                    const T& value)

Copies the range [first, last) to the range that starts at result. Only items that are not equal to value are copied. Items are compared using the == operator. You must ensure the output range is large enough for the result. The return value is an iterator that points to one position past the end of the result range.

Out **remove_copy_if**(Inp first, Inp last, Out result,
                       Pred pred)

Copies the range [first, last) to the range that starts at result. Items are copied only if pred(*iter*) returns false. You must ensure the output range is large enough for the result. The return value is an iterator that points to one position past the end of the result range.

Fwd **remove_if**(Fwd first, Fwd last, Pred pred)

Reorders the range [first, last) to prepare for erasing all elements for which pred(*iter*) returns true. The return value is an iterator such that pred returns false for all elements in the range [first, *return*). Typical usage of remove_if is to erase the removed elements by calling a container's erase(*return*, last) member function, passing remove_if's return value as the first argument to erase.

void **replace**(Fwd first, Fwd last,
                 const T& old_value, const T& new_value)

Replaces all occurrences of old_value with new_value in the range [first, last). Items are compared to old_value with the == operator.

Out **replace_copy**(Inp first, Inp last, Out result,
                const T& old_value, const T& new_value)

Copies the range [first, last) to the range that starts at result. Only items not equal to old_value are copied; items that are equal are replaced with new_value. Items are compared to old_value with the == operator. You must ensure the output range is large enough for the result. The return value is an iterator that points to one position past the end of the result range.

Out **replace_copy_if**(Inp first, Inp last, Out result,
                Pred pred, const T& new_value)

Copies the range [first, last) to the range that starts at result. Only items for which pred(*iter) returns false are copied; items for which pred returns true are replaced with new_value. You must ensure the output range is large enough for the result. The return value is an iterator that points to one position past the end of the result range.

void **replace_if**(Fwd first, Fwd last,
                Pred pred, const T& new_value)

Replaces all values for which pred(*iter) returns true with new_value, in the range [first, last).

void **reverse**(BiDi first, BiDi last)

Reverses the values in the range [first, last) in place.

Out **reverse_copy**(BiDi first, BiDi last, Out result)

Copies the range [first, last) to the range that starts at result, in reverse order. You must ensure the output range is large enough for the result. The return value is an iterator that points to one position past the end of the result range.

void **rotate**(Fwd first, Fwd middle, Fwd last)

Rotates elements in the range [first, last) to the left so that the items in the range [middle, last) are moved to the start of the new sequence. Elements in the range [first, middle) are rotated to the end.

Out **rotate_copy**(Fwd first, Fwd middle, Fwd last,
              Out result)

Copies elements from the range [middle, last) to the
range that starts at result, followed by the elements from
[first, middle), thereby effecting a rotation to the left.
You must ensure the output range is large enough for the
result. The return value is an iterator that points to one
position past the end of the result range.

Fwd2 **swap_ranges**(Fwd1 first1, Fwd1 last1,
                Fwd2 first2)

Swaps all values in the range [first1, last1) with the values in the range that starts at first2 and has the same
length as the first range. You must ensure the output
range is large enough for the result. The return value is
an iterator that points to one position past the end of the
result range.

Out **transform**(Inp first, Inp last,
            Out result, UnOp unop)
Out **transform**(Inp1 first1, Inp1 last1, Inp2 first2,
            Out result, BinOp binop)

Modifies every value in a range by applying a transformation function and assigning the transformed result to the
range that starts at result. You must ensure the output
range is large enough for the result; the output range can
be the same as an input range. The return value is an iterator that points to one position past the end of the result
range.

The first form transforms the input range [first, last) by
calling unop(*iter) for each element in the range.

The second form calls a binary transformation function,
binop(*iter1, *iter2). The first argument, iter1, iterates over [first1, last1). The second argument, iter2,
iterates over the second input range, which starts at
first2 and has the same size as the first input range.

```
Fwd unique(Fwd first, Fwd last)
Fwd unique(Fwd first, Fwd last, BinPred pred)
```
Reorders the range [first, last) to prepare for erasing all adjacent, duplicate items, that is, items for which *iter == *(iter+1). For each sequence of two or more identical items, only the first is kept. The first form compares items for equality with the == operator; the second form calls pred, which must return true for items that are considered equal.

The return value is an iterator that points to one position past the end of the unique items. Typical usage of unique is to erase the removed elements by calling a container's erase(return, last) member function, passing unique's return value as the first argument to erase.

```
Out unique_copy(Inp first, Inp last, Out result)
Out unique_copy(Inp first, Inp last, Out result,
                BinPred pred)
```
Copies the range [first, last) to the range that starts at result. For each sequence of two or more identical items, only the first is copied. The first form compares items for equality with the == operator; the second form calls pred, which must return true for items that are considered equal.

Uninitialized Sequence Operations

These algorithms are declared in <memory> and operate on uninitialized memory. Instead of using assignment, they use placement new to construct copies.

```
Fwd uninitialized_copy(Inp first, Inp last, Fwd result)
```
Copies every item in the range [first, last) to the range that starts at result. You must ensure the output range has enough room for the entire copy. The result range is assumed to be uninitialized, and items are copied by using placement new instead of assignment.

void **uninitialized_fill**(Fwd first, Fwd last, const T& x)
> Fills the range [first, last) with copies of x. The range is assumed to be uninitialized, and it is filled by using placement new instead of assignment.

void **uninitialized_fill_n**(Fwd first, Size n, const T& x)
> Fills the range [first, first+n) with copies of value. The range is assumed to be uninitialized, and it is filled by using placement new instead of assignment.

Sorting

These algorithms are related to sorting and partitioning. You can supply a comparison function or functor, or rely on the default, which uses the < operator.

The complexity of the partitioning and partial sort functions is logarithmic. The complexity of the sort functions is usually $n \log n$, but sort can have worse behavior in the worst case.

void **nth_element**(Rnd first, Rnd nth, Rnd last)
void **nth_element**(Rnd first, Rnd nth, Rnd last,
>   Cmp comp)

> Partitions the range [first, last) so that the value of *nth is what would be at that position if the entire range were sorted. Also, all items in the range [first, nth) are less than or equal to all the items in the range [nth, last). Complexity is linear in the average case, but can be worse in the worst case.

void **partial_sort**(Rnd first, Rnd middle, Rnd last)
void **partial_sort**(Rnd first, Rnd middle, Rnd last,
>   Cmp comp)

> Partitions the range [first, last) so that all the items in [first, middle) are less than or equal to all the items in [middle, last). Also, the range [first, middle) is sorted into ascending order. The first form compares values using the < operator; the second form calls comp(*iter1, *iter2).

```
Rnd partial_sort_copy(Inp first, Inp last,
                      Rnd result_first, Rnd result_last)
Rnd partial_sort_copy(Inp first, Inp last,
                      Rnd result_first, Rnd result_last,
                      Cmp comp)
```
Copies and sorts items from the input range [first, last) to the output range [result_first, result_last). The number of items copied is the smaller of the size of the input range and the size of the output range. Elements are taken from the entire input range, even if it is larger than the output range.

The first form compares values using the < operator; the second form calls comp(*iter1, *iter2).

```
BiDi partition(BiDi first, BiDi last, Pred pred)
```
Reorders the range [first, last) so all items for which pred(*iter) is true come before all items for which the predicate is false.

```
void sort(Rnd first, Rnd last)
void sort(Rnd first, Rnd last, Cmp comp)
```
Sorts the range [first, last) in ascending order. The first form compares values using the < operator; the second form calls comp.

```
BiDi stable_partition(BiDi first, BiDi last, Pred pred)
```
Reorders the range [first, last) so that all items for which pred(*iter) is true come before all items for which the predicate is false. The relative order of items within a partition does not change.

```
void stable_sort(Rnd first, Rnd last)
void stable_sort(Rnd first, Rnd last, Cmp comp)
```
Sorts the range [first, last) in ascending order. The relative order of equivalent items does not change. The first form compares values using the < operator; the second form calls comp.

Merging

These algorithms merge two sorted sequences. Complexity of the merge functions is usually linear, but it can be $n \log n$ if sufficient memory is not available.

```
void inplace_merge(BiDi first, BiDi mid, BiDi last)
void inplace_merge(BiDi first, BiDi mid, BiDi last,
                   Cmp comp)
```

Merges two sorted, consecutive subranges in place, creating a single sorted range. The two ranges are [first, mid) and [mid, last). The resulting range is [first, last). The first form compares values using the < operator; the second form calls comp.

```
Out merge(Inp1 first1, Inp1 last1,
          Inp2 first2, Inp2 last2, Out result)
Out merge(Inp1 first1, Inp1 last1,
          Inp2 first2, Inp2 last2, Out result, Cmp comp)
```

Merges two sorted ranges, copying the results to a separate range. The two ranges are [first1, last1) and [first2, last2). The result range starts at result. You must ensure the output range is large enough for the result. The return value is an iterator that points to one position past the end of the result range. The first form compares values using the < operator; the second form calls comp.

Set Operations

The set algorithms apply standard set operations to sorted sequences. Complexity of the set functions is linear.

```
bool includes(Inp1 first1, Inp1 last1,
              Inp2 first2, Inp2 last2)
bool includes(Inp1 first1, Inp1 last1,
              Inp2 first2, Inp2 last2, Cmp comp)
```

Determines whether the sorted range [first2, last2) is a subset of [first1, last1). In other words, the return value

---

is true if every item in the second range is also present in the first range. Otherwise, the return value is false. The first form compares values using the < operator; the second form calls comp.

```
Out set_difference(Inp1 first1, Inp1 last1,
                   Inp2 first2, Inp2 last2, Out result)
Out set_difference(Inp1 first1, Inp1 last1,Inp2 first2,
                   Inp2 last2, Out result, Cmp comp)
```

Copies the set difference of the sorted range [first1, last1) minus the sorted range [first2, last2) to an output range that starts at result. That is, items are copied from the first range only if they are not present in the second range.

You must ensure the output range is large enough for the result. The return value is an iterator that points to one position past the end of the result range. The first form compares values using the < operator; the second form calls comp.

```
Out set_intersection(Inp1 first1, Inp1 last1,Inp2
                     first2, Inp2 last2, Out result)
Out set_intersection(Inp1 first1, Inp1 last1,Inp2
                     first2, Inp2 last2, Out result,
                     Cmp comp)
```

Copies the set intersection of the sorted range [first1, last1) with the sorted range [first2, last2) to an output range that starts at result. That is, items are copied from the first range only if they are also present in the second range.

You must ensure the output range is large enough for the result. The return value is an iterator that points to one position past the end of the result range. The first form compares values using the < operator; the second form calls comp.

```
Out set_symmetric_difference(Inp1 first1, Inp1 last1,
                             Inp2 first2, Inp2 last2,
                             Out result)
Out set_symmetric_difference(Inp1 first1, Inp1 last1,
                             Inp2 first2, Inp2 last2,
                             Out result, Cmp comp)
```

Copies the set symmetric difference of the sorted range
[first1, last1) with the sorted range [first2, last2) to
an output range that starts at result. That is, items are
copied from both input ranges if they are present in only
one of the input ranges. Items that are in both ranges are
not copied.

You must ensure the output range is large enough for the
result. The return value is an iterator that points to one
position past the end of the result range. The first form
compares values using the < operator; the second form
calls comp.

```
Out set_union(Inp1 first1, Inp1 last1, Inp2 first2,
              Inp2 last2, Out result)
Out set_union(Inp1 first1, Inp1 last1, Inp2 first2,
              Inp2 last2, Out result, Cmp comp)
```

Copies the set union of the sorted range [first1, last1)
with the sorted range [first2, last2) to an output range
that starts at result. That is, items are copied and
merged from both input ranges; items that are present in
both ranges are copied only once to the output range.

You must ensure the output range is large enough for the
result. The return value is an iterator that points to one
position past the end of the result range. The first form
compares values using the < operator; the second form
calls comp.

Heap Operations

These algorithms treat a sequence as a heap data structure. A
C++ heap is a sequence such that the first element is the larg-

est, and inserting or erasing a single element can be performed in logarithmic time.

```
void make_heap(Rnd first, Rnd last)
void make_heap(Rnd first, Rnd last, Cmp comp)
```
> Reorders the range [first, last) into heap order. The
> first form compares values using the < operator; the sec-
> ond form calls comp. Complexity is linear.

```
void pop_heap(Rnd first, Rnd last)
void pop_heap(Rnd first, Rnd last, Cmp comp)
```
> Reorders the range [first, last) to remove the first item
> from the heap. The first item is moved to the end of the
> range, and the remaining items are reordered to heap
> order. Typical usage is to erase the last item after pop-
> ping it from the heap (e.g., by calling a container's pop_
> back member function).
>
> The first form compares values using the < operator; the
> second form calls comp. Complexity is logarithmic.

```
void push_heap(Rnd first, Rnd last)
void push_heap(Rnd first, Rnd last, Cmp comp)
```
> Adds an item to a heap. The heap is in the range [first,
> last - 1), and the item to add is *(last - 1). The item is
> added to the heap, and the range [first, last) is reor-
> dered into heap order. Typical usage is to call a con-
> tainer's push_back member function to add an item, and
> then call push_heap to restore proper heap order.
>
> The first form compares values using the < operator; the
> second form calls comp. Complexity is logarithmic.

```
void sort_heap(Rnd first, Rnd last)
void sort_heap(Rnd first, Rnd last, Cmp comp)
```
> Sorts the items in the range [first, last), which are ini-
> tially in heap order. The first form compares values using
> the < operator; the second form calls comp. Complexity is
> $n \log n$.

Permutations

These algorithms reorder the elements of a sequence to generate permutations. The first permutation is when the sequence is sorted in ascending order; the last permutation is in descending order. Complexity of the permutation functions is linear.

bool **next_permutation**(BiDi first, BiDi last)
bool **next_permutation**(BiDi first, BiDi last, Cmp comp)

> Reorders the range [first, last) to form the next permutation. If the range is already in the last permutation, the first permutation is generated and false is returned. Otherwise, the next permutation is generated and true is returned.
>
> The first form compares values using the < operator; the second form calls comp.

bool **prev_permutation**(BiDi first, BiDi last)
bool **prev_permutation**(BiDi first, BiDi last, Cmp comp)

> Reorders the range [first, last) to form the previous permutation. If the range is already in the first permutation, the last permutation is generated and false is returned. Otherwise, the previous permutation is generated and true is returned.
>
> The first form compares values using the < operator; the second form calls comp.

Miscellaneous

This section lists one algorithm that does not fit in the other categories:

void **swap**(T& a, T& b)

> Swaps the values of a and b. Note that the standard containers overload swap to call the containers' swap member function.

Numerics

The numeric algorithms are declared in the <numeric> header. The T template parameter can be any numeric type. If you define your own type, it must behave similarly to the built-in types. Functions and functors that you pass to the numeric algorithms must not have side effects.

```
T accumulate(Inp first, Inp last, T init)
T accumulate(Inp first, Inp last, T init, BinOp binop)
```
Returns the sum of init plus all the values in the range [first, last). The result and intermediate sum have the same type as init. The first form uses the + operator, and the second version calls binop.

```
OutIter adjacent_difference(Inp first, Inp last,
                            Out result)
OutIter adjacent_difference(Inp first, Inp last,
                            Out result, BinOp binop)
```
Computes the differences of adjacent elements in the range [first, last) and assigns those differences to the output range starting at result. You must ensure the output range is large enough for the result. The result iterator can be the same as first. The return value is an iterator that points to one position past the end of the result range. The first form calls the - operator, and the second form calls binop.

```
T inner_product(Inp1 first1, Inp1 last1,
                Inp2 first2, T init)
T inner_product(Inp1 first1, Inp1 last1,
                Inp2 first2, T init,
                BinOp1 binop1, BinOp2 binop2)
```
Computes an inner product of two ranges by adding the products of corresponding items in [first1, last1) and [first2, *last2*) where *last2* = first2 + (last1 − first1). The first form uses the + and * operators; the second form calls binop1 and binop2, respectively.

```
Out partial_sum(Inp first, Inp last, Out result)
Out partial_sum(Inp first, Inp last, Out result,
                BinOp binop)
```

Assigns partial sums to the range that starts at result. The partial sums are computed by summing successively larger subranges of [first, last). Thus, the first result item is *first, the second is *first + *(first + 1), and so on. You must ensure the output range is large enough for the result. The result iterator can be the same as first. The return value is an iterator that points to one position past the end of the result range. The first form uses the + operator, and the second form calls binop.

Function Objects

The <functional> header defines several *function objects* or *functors*. A function object is an object that has an operator( ), so it can be called using the same syntax as a function.

The standard function objects are defined for C++ operators; for binding function arguments; and for adapting functions, member functions, etc., as function objects.

Using Functors

Functors are most often used with the standard algorithms. For example, to copy a sequence of numbers, adding a fixed amount (42) to each value, you could use the following expression:

```
std::transform(src.begin(), src.end(), dst.begin( ),
               std::bind2nd(std::plus<int>( ), 42))
```

The result of combining bind2nd and plus<int> is a function object that adds the value 42 when it is applied to any integer. The transform algorithm copies all the elements from src to dst, applying the functional argument to each element. For details, see the description of transform in the earlier section, "Algorithms," and bind2nd and plus in this section.

The next few examples will use the Employee class, shown in Example 2.

Example 2. Employee class

```cpp
class Employee {
public:
  Employee(const std::string& name)
    : name_(name), sales_(0)      {}
  int        sales()      const { return sales_; }
  std::string name()      const { return name_; }
  void       make_sale(int n)   { sales_ += n; }
private:
  std::string name_;
  int sales_;
};
```

Suppose you have a vector of Employee objects and you want to find out which employees meet or exceed a sales target. No existing functor lets you call a member function and compare the result with a value, so you need to write your own. Example 3 shows the sales_checker functor, which implements a predicate that tests whether an employee's sales meet or exceed a threshold. The print_good_sales function prints the names of everyone whose sales meet or exceed a threshold.

Example 3. Testing sales

```cpp
class sales_checker :
public std::binary_function<Employee, int, bool> {
public:
  bool operator()(const Employee& e, int threshold)
  const
  {
    return e.sales() >= threshold;
  }
};

void print_good_sales(std::vector<Employee>& emps,
                      int threshold)
{
```

Example 3. Testing sales (continued)

```cpp
  using namespace std;
  remove_copy_if(emps.begin(), emps.end( ),
    ostream_iterator<Employee>(cout, "\n"),
    not1(bind2nd(sales_checker( ), threshold)));
}
```

The standard library lacks the copy_if algorithm, so
Example 3 uses remove_copy_if, which copies elements for
which a predicate returns false. The sales_checker is bound
to the threshold value, and the not1 adapter is used to reverse
the logic, returning true for employees whose sales fell below
the sales threshold.

Functor Foundations

All the functor classes in <functional> derive from binary_
function or unary_function. These class templates take template parameters for the argument and result types, and
declare standard names for those types.

binary_function class template

The binary_function template is a base class template for all
the function classes that represent binary operations. It provides standard names for the argument and result types:

```cpp
    template <typename Arg1, typename Arg2, typename Result>
    struct binary_function {
      typedef Arg1 first_argument_type;
      typedef Arg2 second_argument_type;
      typedef Result result_type;
    };
```

The base template has separate template parameters for each
of the argument types and the return type. Many of the pre-
defined function objects in this section use the same type for
all three parameters, but you can use different types when
defining your own function object.

unary_function class template

The unary_function template is a base class for all the function classes that represent unary operations. It provides standard names for the argument and result types:

```
template <typename Arg, typename Result>
struct unary_function {
  typedef Arg argument_type;
  typedef Result result_type;
};
```

Adapters

The adapters take pointers to functions and pointers to member functions, and adapt them as function objects. The easiest way to use the adapters is to call a function template, which lets the compiler deduce the type of the function or member function pointer. Several different functor class templates are provided, and argument type deduction lets the compiler choose the correct one.

The adapters recognize pointers to member functions of zero or one argument, and pointers to nonmember functions of one or two arguments.

To decide which adapter to use, follow these simple rules:

1. If the function is not a member function or is a static member function, call ptr_fun.

2. If the function is a nonstatic member function, and you are working with objects, call mem_fun_ref, which calls the member function using an object reference.

3. If the function is a nonstatic member function, and you are working with pointers to objects, call mem_fun.

mem_fun function template

The mem_fun<Rtn,T,Arg> function template takes a pointer to a member function as an argument and returns a function object that can call the member function. The function object must be applied to a pointer to T (or a derived class). The Rtn template parameter is the return type of the member function; the T template parameter is the class that has the member function. The optional Arg template parameter is the type of the argument to the member function.

The mem_fun function template is usually the simplest way to create a function object that wraps a member function. In normal use, the compiler deduces the template parameters. The deduced type of the functor class can be any of the following:

```
const_mem_fun_t
const_mem_fun1_t
mem_fun_t
mem_fun1_t
```

All four class templates work similarly by overloading operator( ). The first argument to operator( ) is a pointer to the object whose member function is called. If the member function takes an argument, operator( ) must have a second argument, which is passed to the member function. Otherwise, the member function is called with no arguments. The standard library does not offer adapters for member functions with two or more arguments. See "Boost" for a library extension that is more flexible.

mem_fun_ref function template

The mem_fun_ref function template takes a pointer to a member function as an argument and returns a function object that can call the member function. The function object must be applied to an object of type T (or a derived class). The object is passed by reference to the functor. The Rtn template parameter is the return type of the member function; the T template parameter is the class that has the member function. The optional Arg template parameter is the type of the argument to the member function.

The `mem_fun_ref` function is usually the simplest way to create a function object that wraps a member function. In normal use, the compiler deduces the template parameters. The deduced type of the functor class can be any of the following:

```
const_mem_fun_ref_t
const_mem_fun1_ref_t
mem_fun_ref_t
mem_fun1_ref_t
```

All four class templates work similarly by overloading `operator()`. The first argument to `operator()` is the object whose member function is called. If the member function takes an argument, `operator()` must have a second argument, which is passed to the member function. Otherwise, the member function is called with no arguments. The standard library does not offer adapters for member functions with two or more arguments. See "Boost" for a library extension that is more flexible.

ptr_fun function template

The `ptr_fun` function template creates a function object from a pointer to a function. The compiler deduces the type of the argument, which must be a nonmember function or static member function of one or two arguments. The deduced type of the functor class can be either of the following:

```
pointer_to_binary_function
pointer_to_unary_function
```

Both class templates work similarly by overloading `operator()`. The function to be called must take one or two arguments, and `operator()` takes the same number of arguments, which it passes directly to the function. The standard library does not offer adapters for functions with three or more arguments. See "Boost" for a library extension that is more flexible.

Binders

A binder is a functor of one argument that binds a value as one argument to another functor of two arguments. You can bind a value to the first argument or to the second. A typical use for binders is calling a standard algorithm that requires a one-argument functor.

The easiest way to use a binder is to call one of the binder function templates. The compiler deduces the argument types and chooses an appropriate binder class template. The binder function templates are:

binder1st<Op> **bind1st**(const Op& op, const T& x)
> Binds x to the first argument of op (a two-argument functor) yielding a one-argument functor. When that functor is called with an argument *arg*, it calls op(x, *arg*).

binder2nd<Op> **bind2nd**(const Op& op, const T& x)
> Binds x to the second argument of op yielding a one-argument functor. When that functor is called with an argument *arg*, it calls op(*arg*, x).

Suppose you have a container of data points and you want to count the number of points that exceed a threshold. You can use a standard comparison functor, which takes two arguments, and bind the threshold as one of the arguments. In this case, you can choose to bind the first or the second argument. Use less_equal as the comparator if you bind the first (count the items for which less_equal(threshold, item) is true), or greater if you bind the second (count the items for which greater(item, threshold) is true):

```
// Count values that exceed a threshold.
std::cout
  << std::count_if(data.begin(), data.end( ),
      std::bind1st(std::less_equal<double>( ), threshold))
  << '\n';
// Do the same thing, but this time bind the
// threshold as the second argument.
```

```
std::cout
  << std::count_if(data.begin(), data.end( ),
        std::bind2nd(std::greater<double>( ), threshold))
  << '\n';
```

See also the "Boost" section later in this book, which describes generalized binders that can take any number of arguments.

Arithmetic and Logical Functors

The arithmetic and logical functors are simple class templates that overload operator( ) to perform an arithmetic or logical operation. The bitwise and shift operators are not supplied, but you can easily implement them yourself. The arithmetic and comparison functors have a similar form, which depends on whether the operator is binary or unary. Binary functors look like this:

```
template <typename T>
struct minus : binary_function<T, T, T> {
  T operator( )(const T& x, const T& y) const;
};
```

such that operator( ) returns x operated on y, in this case, x - y. The logical operators do not perform short-circuiting because the operands must be evaluated before operator( ) is called.

Unary functors look like this:

```
template <typename T>
struct negate : unary_function<T,T> {
  T operator( )(const T& x) const;
};
```

such that operator( ) returns the operation on x, in this case, -x.

The following are the binary arithmetic and logical functors, with the operator shown in parentheses:

- divides (/)
- logical_and (&&)
- logical_or (||)

- minus (-)
- modulus (%)
- multiplies (*)
- plus (+)

The unary arithmetic and logical functors are:

- logical_not (!)
- negate (-)

Two additional functors are provided, which apply logical negation to the result of a unary or binary predicate. Two function templates provide a convenient way to construct these functors, letting the compiler deduce the type of the predicate (which can be a function pointer or a function object):

```
template <typename Predicate>
unary_negate<Predicate> not1(const Predicate& pred)
```
> Returns a unary functor, for which operator( ) returns the logical negation of calling pred(x). The functor type is unary_negate.

```
template <typename Predicate>
binary_negate<Predicate> not2(const Predicate& pred)
```
> Returns a binary functor, for which operator( ) returns the logical negation of calling pred(x, y). The functor type is binary_negate.

Comparison Functors

The comparison functors are simple class templates that overload operator( ) to perform a relational or equality comparison. A frequently used comparison functor is less, which is the default comparator for associative containers. (See the "Containers" section earlier in this book.)

All the comparison functors have the same form:

```
template <typename T>
struct equal_to : binary_function<T, T, bool> {
  bool operator()(const T& x, const T& y) const;
};
```

such that operator() returns the comparison of x with y, in this case, x == y.

The following are the comparison functors, with the operator shown in parentheses:

- equal_to (==)
- greater (>)
- greater_equal (>=)
- less (<)
- less_equal (<=)
- not_equal_to (!=)

Miscellaneous

This section describes allocator, auto_ptr, and bitset—class templates that don't quite fit in the other sections.

Allocators

An allocator is an abstraction of the new and delete expressions. The standard containers use allocators to allocate and free memory, and to construct and destroy objects that reside in a container.

The standard library defines the allocator class template, which is the default allocator for every standard container. You can supply a different allocator as long as it provides the same interface as the standard allocator.

Implementing a new allocator is trickier than it seems at first and is beyond the scope of this book. This section describes how to use the standard allocator class template.

The following are the member types of allocator:

typedef const T* **const_pointer**
    A type for a pointer to const.

typedef const T& **const_reference**
    A type for a const lvalue.

typedef ptrdiff_t **difference_type**
    A type to represent the difference of any two pointers
    that the allocator returns from allocate( ).

typedef T* **pointer**
    A pointer type.

template <class U> struct **rebind**
    Binds the allocator object to a different value type. The
    rebind class has a single typedef, other, which is an
    instance of allocator, but with U as the template parame-
    ter. The rebind template is necessary for standard con-
    tainers that allocate helper objects, such as link nodes,
    rather than allocating values directly. If you are not
    implementing a standard container, you probably don't
    need to understand rebind.

typedef T& **reference**
    An lvalue type.

typedef size_t **size_type**
    A type that can represent the size of the largest alloca-
    tion request.

typedef T **value_type**
    The type of allocated values.

The following are the member functions of allocator:

allocator() throw( )
allocator(const allocator&) throw( )
template<class U> **allocator**(const allocator<U>&) throw( )
    Constructs a new allocator object, possibly copying an
    existing allocator.

---

pointer **address**(reference x) const
const_pointer **address**(const_reference x) const
Returns the address of x, that is, &x.

pointer **allocate**(size_type n,allocator<void>::
                      const_pointer hint = 0)
Calls the global operator new to allocate enough memory
to hold n objects of type T. The hint argument must be 0
or a pointer obtained from a prior call to allocate that
has not yet been passed to deallocate. The return value
is a pointer to the newly allocated memory. If the memory cannot be allocated, bad_alloc is thrown.

void **construct**(pointer p, const T& val)
Constructs a copy of val at address p, using global placement new.

void **deallocate**(pointer p, size_type n)
Calls the global operator delete to free the memory that
p points to. The n argument is the number of items of
type T—the same value passed to allocate.

void **destroy**(pointer p)
Calls the destructor for the object at address p. That is, it
calls reinterpret_cast<T*>(p)->~T( ).

size_type **max_size**( ) const throw( )
Returns the maximum size that can be passed to
allocate.

The standard defines the allocate<void> template specialization, which does not declare allocate, construct, and so on,
because you cannot create an object of type void. You can,
however, refer to the pointer, const_pointer, and rebind
members.

The equality operators (operator== and operator!=) are overloaded so an allocator object is equal to all other allocator
objects regardless of the value type.

Bitset

A bitset is a packed, fixed-size sequence of bits. It is not a standard container, and it does not support iterators.

The bitset class template takes a single template parameter, N, which specifies the number of bits. It is declared in the <bitset> header.

A bit can be *set* (one) or *reset* (zero). *Flipping* a bit means to toggle a one to a zero or a zero to a one. The following are the members of bitset:

bitset( )
>   Constructs the bitset with all bits reset.

bitset(unsigned long value)
>   Constructs the bitset, initializing the first m bits to value, in which m == CHAR_BITS * sizeof(unsigned long). If $N > m$, all other bits are reset. If $N < m$, excess bits of m are ignored.

template<typename CharT, typename Traits, typename Alc>
explicit **bitset**(const basic_string<CharT,Traits,Alc>& s, typename basic_string<CharT,Traits,Alc>::size_type p=0, typename basic_string <CharT,Traits,Alc>::size_type n= basic_string<CharT,Traits,Alc>::npos)

>   Constructs the bitset, initializing it from the character string s, starting at index p, and extending for n characters (or to the end of the string, whichever comes first). The default is to use all characters in the string. A character equal to '0' resets a bit, '1' sets a bit, and any other character causes the constructor to throw invalid_argument.

>   The rightmost character of the substring (that is, the character s[p+n-1] or the rightmost character of s) initializes the least-significant bit at index 0 of the bitset, and subsequent bits are initialized by characters at preceding indices of s. Bits left uninitialized by the string are reset.

All of the bitsets in the following example are equal to 000111:

```
bitset<6> a(string("111"));
bitset<6> b(string("000111"));
bitset<6> c(string("10110011100"), 5, 4);
bitset<6> d(string("111111"), 3, 42);
```

The unwieldy declaration is due to the basic_string class template. For the common case of a plain string, you can read the declaration as:

```
bitset(const string& s, size_t p=0,
        size_t n=string::npos)
```

bool **any**( ) const
Returns true if any bit is set. Returns false if all bits are zero.

size_t **count**( ) const
Returns the number of bits set.

bitset<N>& **flip**( )
Toggles all bits. Returns *this.

bitset<N>& **flip**(size_t pos)
Toggles the bit at position pos. If pos is invalid, throws out_of_range. Returns *this.

bool **none**( ) const
Returns true if all bits are reset. Returns false if any bit is set.

reference **operator[]**(size_t pos)
Returns a bitset::reference object for the bit at position pos. The behavior is undefined if pos is out of range. The bitset::reference class is a proxy that holds a reference to the bitset object and pos. It overloads the assignment operator so assignments to the reference object modify the bitset. The reference class also defines a member function, flip( ), to toggle the referenced bit.

```
bool operator[](size_t pos) const
```
Returns the value of the bit at position pos. The behavior is undefined if pos is out of range.

```
bitset<N>& reset()
```
Resets all bits. Returns *this.

```
bitset<N>& reset(size_t pos)
```
Resets the bit at position pos. If pos is invalid, throws out_of_range. Returns *this.

```
bitset<N>& set()
```
Sets all bits. Returns *this.

```
bitset<N>& set(size_t pos, int val = true)
```
Sets the bit at position pos to val != 0. If pos is invalid, throws out_of_range. Returns *this.

```
size_t size() const
```
Returns N.

```
bool test(size_t pos) const
```
Returns the value of the bit at position pos. Throws out_of_range if pos is invalid.

```
template <class charT, class traits, class Allocator>
basic_string<charT, traits, Allocator> to_string() const
```
Returns a string representation of the bitset. Each bit is converted to the character '0' if reset or '1' if set. Bit position 0 is the rightmost character (position N − 1).

The compiler cannot deduce the template parameters when calling to_string, so you must specify them explicitly:

```
std::bitset<64> bits(std::
string("101000111101010101"));
std::string str =
  bits.template to_string<char, std::char_traits<char>,
                   std::allocator<char> >());
```

```
unsigned long to_ulong() const
```
Returns the integral value of the bitset. Throws overflow_error if N is too large for unsigned long.

All the bitwise, shift, and equality operators are also defined for bitset, with the usual semantics. The operands of the binary operators must have the same size. The shift operators fill vacated bits with zero bits.

The I/O operators are also overloaded. The output operator<< writes a bitset as a string using the same format as the to_string function. The input operator>> reads a bitset from a string using the same format as the constructor.

Pairs

The pair class template represents a pair of related objects. The most common use for pairs is by the map and multimap class templates, which store pairs of keys and associated objects. The <utility> header declares pair and related function templates.

The declaration of pair is mostly self-explanatory:

```
template <typename T1, typename T2>
struct pair {
  typedef T1 first_type;
  typedef T2 second_type;
  T1 first;
  T2 second;
  pair();
  pair(const T1& x, const T2& y);
  template<typename U, typename V>
    pair(const pair<U, V> &p);
};
```

The pair<T1,T2> constructors are straightforward:

pair( )
    Initializes first as T1( ) and second as T2( ).

pair(const T1& x, const T2& y)
    Initializes first with x and second with y.

```
template<typename U, typename V>
```
pair(const pair<U, V> &p)

> Initializes first with p.first and second with p.second, performing implicit conversions as needed.

Several function templates make it easier for you to work with pairs:

```
template <typename T1, typename T2>
```
pair<T1,T2> **make_pair**(T1 a, T2 b)

> Constructs a pair<T1,T2> object and initializes it with the values a and b. The advantage of using make_pair over a simple pair<> constructor is that the compiler can deduce the types T1 and T2 from the values a and b.

```
template <typename T1, typename T2>
```
bool **operator==**(const pair<T1,T2>& a, const pair<T1,T2>& b)

> Returns true if a and b are equal, that is, a.first == b.first && a.second == b.second.

```
template <typename T1, typename T2>
```
bool **operator<**(const pair<T1,T2>& a, const pair<T1,T2>& b)

> Returns true if a is less than b, assuming the first member is more significant than the second. That is, the return value is a.first < b.first || (!(b.first < a.first) && a.second < b.second).

The other comparison operators are defined in terms of operator== and operator<.

Smart Pointer

The auto_ptr class template (in the <memory> header) implements a smart pointer for ownership of pointers. Proper use of auto_ptr ensures that a pointer has exactly one owner (which prevents accidental double deletes), and the owner automatically frees the memory when the owner goes out of scope (which prevents memory leaks). Assignment of auto_ptr values transfers ownership from the source to the target of the assignment.

The following are the members of auto_ptr<T>:

typedef T **element_type**
A synonym for the base type.

explicit **auto_ptr**(T* p = 0) throw( )
Initializes the auto_ptr object to own the pointer p.

auto_ptr(auto_ptr& x) throw( )
template<class U> **auto_ptr**(auto_ptr<U>& x) throw( )
Initializes the auto_ptr object with the pointer returned from x.release( ). In the second version, the type U* must be implicitly convertible to T*. Note that x is not const. It is not possible to copy a const auto_ptr because to do so would break the ownership rules.

auto_ptr(auto_ptr_ref<T> r) throw( )
Initializes the auto_ptr object with the pointer obtained from calling release on r's auto_ptr.

~auto_ptr( ) throw( )
Deletes the owned pointer, e.g., delete get( ).

T* **get**( ) const throw( )
Returns the owned pointer.

T* **release**( ) throw( )
Returns get( ) and resets the owned pointer to 0.

void **reset**(T* p = 0) throw( )
Deletes the owned pointer (if it is not equal to p) and saves p as the new owned pointer.

```
template<class U> operator auto_ptr_ref<U>() throw()
```
Returns a temporary auto_ptr_ref object that owns the pointer. The pointer must be convertible to U*. Ownership is released and transferred to the new auto_ptr_ref object.

The auto_ptr_ref type is implementation-defined and facilitates using auto_ptr as a function return type. In most cases, you can ignore auto_ptr_ref and simply declare function parameters and return types using auto_ptr, and let the compiler work its magic.

```
template<class U> operator auto_ptr<U>() throw()
```
Returns a new auto_ptr object. The owned pointer is converted to type U*, and ownership is transferred to the new auto_ptr object.

```
auto_ptr& operator=(auto_ptr& x) throw()
template<class U>
auto_ptr& operator=(auto_ptr<U>& x) throw()
auto_ptr& operator=(auto_ptr_ref<T> r) throw()
```
Transfers ownership of the pointer that is owned by x or by the auto_ptr object held by r to *this. That is, it calls reset(x.release()).

```
T& operator*() const throw()
```
Returns *get(). If the owned pointer is a null pointer, the behavior is undefined.

```
T* operator->() const throw()
```
Returns get().

See the "Boost" section below for information about other smart pointers, including smart pointers that can point to arrays and be stored in containers.

Boost

The Boost project is an open source suite of C++ libraries. It is a large project, with libraries for such diverse tasks as creating mathematical graphs, writing parsers, managing threads and concurrency, numerical programming, interfacing with the Python programming language, and so on.

What makes Boost interesting with respect to this book are additional containers, iterator adapters, and the library of function objects. This section briefly introduces Boost containers, function objects, and smart pointers; for details see the Boost web site at *http://www.boost.org*.

All Boost identifiers are declared in the boost namespace. The boost:: scope prefix is omitted from the following descriptions, for the sake of brevity.

NOTE

As I write this book, the C++ standardization committee is preparing a Technical Report (TR1) detailing extensions to the standard library. Some Boost libraries have been accepted into TR1, and others will most likely be accepted at future committee meetings. TR1 will not be normative, that is, library vendors will not be required to implement the library extensions, although most vendors probably will. Thus, you can think of this section as a preview of TR1.

Just as the original STL evolved during the process of standardization, so too will the Boost libraries. At the very least, the header names will change, as will the namespace name. Visit the book's web site (*http://www. tempest-sw.com/cpp*) for up-to-date information about TR1 and how it affects these Boost libraries.

Arrays

The array class template is a fixed-size array that meets most of the requirements of a sequence container. The header is <boost/array.hpp>. The value type is the first template parameter, and the array size is the second parameter:

```
boost::array<int, 10> nums = { 10, 20 };
std::copy(nums.begin(), nums.end(),
  std::ostream_iterator<int>(std::cout, ", "));
```

The array object is not dynamically allocated. In the previous example, nums is an automatic variable. Because no internal pointers to dynamic memory are used, the swap member function has linear performance. This and other design trade-offs are discussed in the Boost documentation.

Dynamic Bitsets

The dynamic_bitset class template (declared in <boost/dynamic_bitset.hpp>) is similar to the standard bitset, except the size can change at runtime. You can provide template arguments that determine the type (default is unsigned long) used to store the packed bits and the allocator (default is std::allocator).

The same member functions and operators are declared in dynamic_bitset as in bitset, plus additional functions for managing the number of bits. The usual bitwise and shift operators are also defined. One major difference between the standard bitset and Boost's dynamic_bitset is that dynamic_bitset does not throw an exception for out-of-range indices, but uses assert to abort the program.

Binders

The Boost binder library (declared in the header <boost/bind.hpp>) generalizes the standard bind1st and bind2nd function templates.

The bind function template is overloaded to bind a wide variety of functions and arguments. You can use pointers to member functions or to nonmember functions. You can bind multiple arguments at the same time, and choose which arguments to bind.

For example, suppose you have a function that generates random integers within a range given by two arguments:

```
int random(int from, int to)
{
  return rand % (to - from + 1) + from;

}
```

You can bind a specific value to both arguments. The result is a function object whose operator( ) takes no arguments. You typically use the resulting function object with a standard algorithm. For example, fill a vector with random throws of a die by calling a functor that binds 1 to from and 6 to to in repeated calls to random:

```
std::generate(vec.begin(), vec.end( ),
              bind(random, 1, 6));
```

You can choose to bind only some of the arguments. Use _1, _2, etc., as placeholders to indicate which arguments of the resulting functor are bound to which arguments of random. That is, _1 is replaced by the first argument to the new functor, _2 by the second, and so on. (Code that uses placeholders is much easier to read if you employ a using directive. Instead of boost::_1, use a plain and simple _1.) You can pass _1, _2, etc., as arguments to the bound function or functor, even repeating an argument. For example, to swap the order of two arguments to the two-argument function f, use bind(f, _2, _1). To replace every element of a vector with a random number between 1 and the element:

```
std::transform(vec.begin(), vec.end( ),
               vec.begin( ),
               bind(random, 1, _1));
```

You can also use bind with other function objects, but you must specify the return type of operator( ) as a template parameter. For example, store a series of bool values that indicate whether the items in a vector are negative:

```
std::transform(vec.begin(), vec.end( ),
               result.begin( ),
               bind<bool>(std::less<int>, _1, 0));
```

Composition

One of the problems with the standard functors is that they have a limited ability to compose multiple functors into a single functor. The Boost library offers several general ways to compose functions and function objects, as declared in the <boost/compose.hpp> header. Table 2 shows the ways functions can be composed.

Table 2. Composing functions or function objects

Function	Boost composer name
f(g( ))	compose_f_g
f(g(x))	compose_f_gx
f(g(x, y))	compose_f_gxy
f(g(x), h(x))	compose_f_gx_hx
f(g(x), h(y))	compose_f_gx_hy

To use a composer, pass two or three function pointers or function objects to the appropriate composer function template. The result is a function object whose operator( ) takes zero, one, or two arguments, depending on the types of *f*, *g*, and *h*. For example, to fill a vector with the results of random throws of two dice, you can start with the function random_1, which takes an integer argument and returns a random integer. Use random_1 as the *g* and *h* functions. To add the two random values, use a standard plus functor. To fill the vector, bind the composed function to 6 (the maximum value for one die):

```
// Return a random integer in the range [1, x].
int random_1(int x)
{
  return random(1, x);
}

int main( )
{
  using namespace boost;
```

```
std::vector<int> vec;
vec.resize(10);
std::generate(vec.begin(), vec.end( ),
  bind(compose_f_gx_hx(std::plus<int>( ),
                       std::ptr_fun(random_1),
                       std::ptr_fun(random_1)),
       6));
...
}
```

Adapters

The mem_fn adapter (in the <boost/mem_fn.hpp> header) is a generalization of the standard mem_fun and mem_fun_ref adapters. Boost's mem_fn adapter can also refer to data members and to member functions with more than one argument. You can refer to objects via reference, ordinary pointers, or smart pointers. Pass the pointer-to-member as the sole argument to mem_fn, which returns a functor.

Boost also has a generic function wrapper (declared in the <boost/function.hpp> header). You can use the function template to hold references to arbitrary function pointers or function objects. The sole template parameter is the signature of the function to be wrapped. Thus, another way to fill a vector with the results of random dice throws is:

```
function<int(int,int)> rnd(std::ptr_fun(random));
function<int(int)> rnd_1 = bind(rnd, 1, _1);
function<int(int)> add_random =
  compose_f_gx_hx(std::plus<int>( ), rnd_1, rnd_1);
function<int( )> throw_dice = bind(add_random, 6);
std::generate(vec.begin(), vec.end( ), throw_dice);
```

Functional Header Replacement

The Boost project has its own version of the standard <functional> header, namely <boost/functional.hpp>. The Boost version offers the same function and class templates, but with a little more flexibility. The most significant change is avoiding the problem of references to references.

If you try to use a standard adapter with a function that uses references for its parameters, the standard adapters fail to compile. The standard adapters pass their arguments as references to const, resulting in a reference to a reference, which is not allowed. Boost uses template tricks to detect and avoid this problem.

Lambda Functions

If you find composers, adapters, and binders to be difficult to read and write, you are not alone. Boost offers its lambda function library as an alternative. This library offers a kind of functional programming in C++. It is too extensive and complicated to explain here, but I offer a single example to demonstrate the expressive power of the Boost lambda library. Like the earlier examples, it fills a vector with the results of random throws of two dice:

```
using namespace boost::lambda;
std::generate(vec.begin(), vec.end(),
  (bind(std::rand) % 6) + (bind(std::rand) % 6) + 2);
```

The bind function in the lambda library takes a function and defers calling the function until the entire lambda expression is evaluated. The arithmetic operators are overloaded, again to defer evaluation. The entire lambda expression is compiled as a functor, and the generate algorithm calls the functor to fill the vector. Each call to the lambda function calls the bound std::rand functions, evaluates the operators, and computes the value for the dice. You do not need the wrapper random or random_1 functions, and you do not need composers, binders, or adapters.

Smart Pointers

Boost has several smart pointer class templates. They solve a number of problems that the standard auto_ptr<> class template does not. For example, you cannot store an auto_ptr<> object in a standard container, but you can store a boost::

shared_ptr<> object. Another limitation of auto_ptr is that it stores a scalar pointer, so you cannot use it with arrays. Boost has shared_array<> to solve that problem. The Boost shared pointer class templates use a reference count to keep track of shared references to the pointer. When the last owner goes out of scope, the memory is freed.

The weak_ptr class template holds a weak pointer to a shared_ptr object. The weak_ptr object does not affect shared_ptr's reference count. A typical use for a weak pointer is in a debugging package: the debugging code can keep track of pointers and display information about them without affecting the normal lifetime of the shared pointers.

If you want automatic lifetime management without the complexity of sharing ownership, use scoped_ptr (for scalars) or scoped_array (for arrays). A scoped pointer does not allow any copying or assignment. The memory is freed when the scoped object goes out of scope. A scoped pointer is handy for local, temporary objects, or for data members that are never exposed publicly.

Each of the Boost smart pointer templates is defined in a header of the same name, e.g., <boost/shared_ptr.hpp> and <boost/scoped_array.hpp>.

Index

We'd like to hear your suggestions for improving our indexes. Send email to
index@oreilly.com.
